FREEDOM OF EXPRESSION UNDER CRIMINAL LAW

PRITHIVI RAJ & HARSHITA VERMA

FREEDOM OF EXPRESSION IN CRIMINAL LAW

By:

PRITHIVI RAJ

Assistant Professor (Law)

Narsee Monjee Institute of Management Studies

(NMIMS) Deemed-to-be-University, Hyderabad Campus

And

HARSHITA VERMA

Narsee Monjee Institute of Management Studies

(NMIMS) Deemed-to-be-University, Hyderabad Campus

Contents

Notion Press Publishing Pvt. Ltd.

Notion Press, Inc.
800, West EI Camino Real #180,
California USA 94040
Notion Press Media Pvt Ltd,
No.50, Chettiyar Agaram Main Road,
Vanagaram, Chennai, Tamil Nadu 600095

Online Available at:

https://notionpress.com/store

Preface

With the recent events involving slogans condemning the death penalty of a terrorist, involving aggressive language and paraphernalia further slamming allegations that there is a widespread miscarriage of justice in India; the issue of hate speech has risen to the front burner and gives rise to the problem: Is Hate speech protected speech?

In 2015, the Supreme Court had struck down Section 66A of the Information Technology Act citing that it violated the fundamental right to free speech. It disproportionately violated the balance between the rights and the restrictions imposed on the exercise of such rights. When it comes to online hate speech, lack of legislation paves the way for infringement of fundamental freedoms of the citizens and the users. Written words may be sent that may be purely in the realm of advocacy of a particular point of view. Furthermore, the mere causing of annoyance, inconvenience, danger, etc. or being grossly offensive, or having a menacing character does not have any penalty under the Indian Penal code. Lack of legislation and the lack of implementation of the existing legislation by the authorities hampers the right to speech and expression or it lets the hatred spread in the society due to it not being penalized. Is the existing legal framework able to tackle the issue of hate speech?

There is an existing problem with regard to dissenting opinions expressed in the public sphere. The Right to freedom of speech and expression also includes the speech that we dislike, that we don't want to hear. The rationale all harmless speech is absolutely protected and all speech is harmless when there is time for more speech to rebut it. The theory is that the remedy for bad speech, hate speech, incendiary speech, and for speech that makes you want to kill the speaker is not to remain silent but to challenge such speaker with more speech, with better reasoning because that is the essence of free speech and expression. Accommodating dissent, welcoming it, and resolving disputes on an intellectual platform. But the Indian society is somewhere still in its colonial mind frame and it poses a problem for the modern Indian society that consists of even more diversities than those that existed at the time of Independence. Are we as a billion-strong nation ready to accommodate the dissenting opinions?

In order to ascertain the problem of Hate Speech and Sedition Laws in India, we have to search for solutions through history surrounding the incorporation of sedition laws and hate speech laws in our country. Whether the existing legislations are sufficient enough to tackle the menace of hate speech and its ever-increasing forms is something that has been ascertained in this work. Is enforcement of sedition laws pervading the citizen's right to freedom of speech and expression?

It is the duty of the State to protect its citizens and above all the feeling of oneness amongst citizens. The Police are the most visible form of State should perform its duty to protect the speaker and the audience, so that the speaker can speak and audience can hear and react. But when the Police serving under immense political atmosphere and pressure, abdicates itself of its primary duty of maintaining law and order, then the audience wants to kill the speaker or the supporters of the speaker want to attack the audience. Tolerance and patience will win the day and not censorship. Is India, as a modern democratic country able to provide protection to minorities?

Prithivi Raj
Harshita Verma

CHAPTER ONE

INTRODUCTION

What makes India special? Is it the fact that we even after centuries of being ruled by various rulers and colonists are still striving to be the greatest democracy of the world or is it the fact that even after multitudes of diversities that exist, we are still standing strong. If not strong, we as one nation want to display our unity in the grimmest of times. India achieved independence on 15th of August 1947, two years after the surrender of one of the greatest axis powers, Japan. In reality we did really achieve our independence only on 26th January 1950, the day our Constitution came into being. It was the time that on one hand we witnessed the goriest acts of violence and on the other hand, the longest Constitution was being framed by the Constituent Assembly. At this assembly's hand was the vital task of taking in the extremes of opinions of its members keeping in mind the: at risk social, dead economical and fused political structure of the country.

The foundation had to be laid down on the basis that the Constitution either remains the same or it transforms. The Constitution aimed at achieving an egalitarian society while simultaneously striving to achieve stability and unity. It ultimately tried to adapt the British India scenario into the newly independent India. There was both, colonial continuity and transformation, to which Constituent Assembly member, K. Hanumanthaiya remarked: "*We wanted the music of veena or sitar, but here we have the music of an English band*".[1] The heart of the Constitution or as it is known, the Fundamental Rights were rights that for first in India's history delivered individualistic rights which were mostly seen in Western countries.

Amongst those pious rights there is: Right to Free Speech and Expression, one of the six fundamental freedoms guaranteed under Article

19 and is contained under Article 19(1) (a). It is subject to restrictions under Article 19(2). Even during colonial times, right to free speech was never given any statutory basis but it was present under British India as a common law right to express oneself. It was subject to four restrictions: Sedition (included in its ambit Hate Speech), Obscenity, Contempt of Court and Defamation.

Free Speech is one of the most cherished rights of mankind yet controversial at the same time. The use or abuse of free speech has resulted in various reactions from the listeners or the targeted audience and also from the administrators. While some promote absolute free speech, others are apprehensive about there being no restrictions on freedom to express oneself as the ultimate end to any expression is the reaction arising from the expressed words, etc. It sometimes may receive violent reactions thereby defeating the very purpose of this freedom.

Our ability to communicate with other beings makes us different from the rest of the living creatures. Therefore the right to freedom of expression has to be monitored carefully, both by the one exercising this right and also by the State. People have plethora of opinions that are affected by various individualistic factors. These factors cause people to have difference of opinion over a specific topic and it thereby can lead either to constructive work or can result in the worst: Violence. Thus, there exists the necessity for regulation of speech. Speech sometimes delivered by countrymen against the government can lead to incitement of violence and such speech can be tried under the offence of Sedition. Hate Speech and Sedition have been closely linked to each other, but in reality this isn't the real picture.

1.1 Sedition Laws in India

British India had a contracted definition of Sedition while England had a more wide definition of the same. In England since 1832, Sedition meant insurrection against government or inciting violence. In England, it was just a misdemeanour, an offence which did not attract stringent punishment and was a bailable offence. It therefore meant that accused as a matter of right could be released on bail and the case against him was scarcely prosecuted. The major reason for holding back prosecution was that the offence was tried in front of a jury that comprised of their own countrymen and therefore conviction was difficult due to sympathetic sentiments.[2]

British India in contrast to the above humane approach had defined Sedition in a very wide manner and included within its ambit even the mere promotion of hatred, disloyalty or bad feelings against the government. Present under Section 124A of Indian Penal Code, 1860, this offence was punishable with transportation, often to Jail stationed at Andaman and Nicobar Islands. While in England, Sedition was punishable with an imprisonment of two years, in India it attracts a graver punishment which may extend to life imprisonment. Indian stance with relation to prosecution was very stringent and the jury included mostly Englishmen and sparsely any Indians. Such is evident by the conviction of Bal Gangadhar Tilak for Sedition in Bombay High Court in which the jury consisted of seven Englishmen and only two Indians. He ultimately was held guilty by 6-3 majority.[3]

1.1.1 Sedition as per Macaulay's Draft

The Indian Penal Code was prepared by the team of four law commission personnel's with Thomas Macaulay as one of the most prominent members. In 1837, he presented the code which under section 113 mentioned an offence by person if he 'excites feelings of disaffection to the government'. This provision was however never brought until the act came into force in 1860. During this period, in 1846 wherein the law commission's certain members presented its report stated their disliking towards sedition as an offence under IPC. This was objected as the provision appeared vague and any unimportant or menial slander against the government could set in course the action based on this provision leading to imprisonment for life and an undefined fine. However, a large of commission's member supported Macaulay's draft and did not object to this provision.[4]

Furthermore, his draft mentioned that criticism which may be extreme or strong or even hostile was not penalised but was only done in the case that such criticism leads to incitement to violence by the audience to such criticism.[5]

1.1.2 Amendment in 1870

It was clear that the Wahabi movement had created problems for the British in India and the jihad carried on was of great concern for the Britishers. Therefore, the law of Sedition was brought forth as a means to curb this movement. Macaulay's provision for Sedition did not see the light of the day in 1860 code as a mistake while drafting was made and somehow was left out while drafting. Sir James Fitzjames Stephen in August 1870 brought forth an amendment recommending the insertion of the left out Section 113. But he had cautioned the Council that criticism sometimes might be used in a normal tone but the audience gathered may be in a mood to create ruckus. He compared the application of Sedition law with the criminal defamation law under section 499 IPC and hoped that it would be applied at par with the latter. Hence, Section 124-A came into being as an offence that could be tried only upon affirmation by the government and not merely upon a complaint. It was a non cognizable as well as non bailable offence while misdemeanours in England continued to be bailable offence.[6]

1.1.3 Bose and Tilak

In 1897, *Jogendra Chandra Bose*[7] was prosecuted for the offence of Sedition and came to be known as the first instance with regard to this offence. He carried out the weekly paper by the name of '*Bangobasi*' which had criticised the role of British government in encroaching upon the Hindu religion as they brought forth the Age of Consent Bill. This bill raised the age of consent for sexual intercourse amongst females from ten years to twelve years and raised eyebrows from every nook and corner of the Indian Hindu community.[8]

Chief Justice W.C. Petheram tried this case and laid down the meaning of word 'disaffection'. He held that it is a feeling opposite to affection and is comparable to the feeling of hatred or disliking. For him Seditious act took place when the speaker has tried to put into the minds of the listeners a feeling to not obey the laws and rule of the government and to even resist the power. The jury was not able reach a unanimous verdict and Jogendra Bose was let out on bail and the case was eventually never decided to reach a conclusive verdict.[9]

In the case of *Bal Gangadhar Tilak*[10], Tilak was editor of the weekly '*Kesari*' which had published an article: '*Shivaji's Utterances*'. The article brought forward a fictional parallel by citing the great 17th century leader Shivaji as he would have looked at the gruesome situation under British Rule and would have reflected upon his time where he established Swarajya. It did not incite or create any public disorder and as per the facts of the case it would have not been able to secure a conviction in England. Justice

Strachey delivered a very controversial judgment where he had nearly put the conviction into the minds of the jury. He had explained Sedition in a very broad term by citing that disaffection meant 'absence of affection' and also 'every possible bad feeling to the government'. He clearly deviated from the English law of Seditious libel and held that incitement to violence or any occurrence of such likely event is immaterial and the onus is mainly if the criticism of the government led to people questioning its motives or feelings towards people. Criticism in harsh and violent manner would constitute the offence of sedition and instructed jury to read in whole of the text and not just certain paragraphs. Ultimately, Tilak was convicted for sedition and sentenced to eighteen months rigorous imprisonment but was released a year later.[11]

In the following years, Sedition was charged in many cases in a high handed manner. In *Ramchandra Narayan*[12] and *Amba Prasad*[13], the definition of Sedition was broadened to great extent and it included every bit of criticism towards the colonial rule. Disaffection had now been equated to disloyalty and hence led to swift conviction. Narayan had issued a paper in Satara called '*Pratod*' which was carrying an article mentioning about preparation for becoming independent from British India and quoted about Canadian people and their manner of life under British. He said that Indians were being subject to cruel in inhuman treatment while the Canadians were given better treatment. For this he was charged with sedition as the readers were being asked to cast off the Britishers in India as they (Englishmen) were foreigners.[14]

1.2 Constituent Assembly on Freedom of Speech and Expression

The Sub-Committee on Fundamental Rights discussed on granting the freedom of speech and expression and the restrictions imposed upon such usage. Drafts of two prominent members, Munshi[15] and Dr. B.R. Ambedkar have noted upon this issue. While Munshi suggested that exercise of such right should be within certain limits and in accordance with the law of Union. B.R. Ambedkar held that no law should be made that restricts the right of free speech except in cases that deal with public order and morality. This right was a part of clause (9) of the draft and it attracted restrictions on the grounds of public order and morality.[16]

1.2.1 Hate Speech

Furthermore, it was Alladi Krishnaswami Ayyar who apprehended the committee on the issue of 'class hatred'. Section 153A[17] of Indian Penal Code, 1860 contains provisions related to class hatred. He wanted the members to realise that restrictions did not find the issue of class hatred and only public order and morality was being cast upon and class hatred should find its place within the restrictions on free speech keeping in mind the violence existing at that time. On this point, he thus suggested the inclusion of emergency as a restriction upon the exercise of this right.[18]

K T Shah expressed his dissent on the use of 'public order' and 'morality' as a restriction upon free speech. He termed these as vague as public order and morality are dynamic concepts. He stressed on defining morality or to drop it completely as India is a country with diverse religions, hence it was difficult to constitute what morality is since it would vary from class to another.[19]

On another meeting, Alladi Krishnaswami Ayyar was supported by Rajagopalachari on the inclusion of class hatred as one of the restrictions as India could progress if there is communal harmony. Syama Prasad Mookerjee, Munshi and Bakshi Tek Chand were opposed to this view and hence rejected this contention. They rejected it on their contention that such restriction could be abused by any political party in power if it is opposed, by terming such opposition as class hatred or communal. Tek Chand was of the opinion that Section 153A was one of the misused sections and cited one example whereby Police force was construed as a class and a newspaper which criticised police action was prosecuted under this section for promoting class hatred.[20]

1.2.2 Sedition

Sedition was used as a tool for curbing the freedom movement leaders of India during colonial times. Their convictions were plagued with procedural impropriety and often led to greater punishment than required. Munshi was a strong advocate of freedom of speech and hence he swiftly moved a motion to eliminate sedition as a restriction from freedom of speech. He cited the federal court case whereas it had been overruled by the Privy Council judgment. He did not support any class of citizens making seditious speeches but he insisted upon sedition being read in a narrow manner unlike broad manner during British times. Other leaders such as Seth Govind Das, Pandit Thakur Das and Rohini Chaudhari also supported the view that sedition be deleted as an exception to free speech.[21]

The above position was necessary for the amalgamation of more than five hundred princely states in India during the newly achieved independence. States such as Junagarh, Hyderabad and Kashmir were problematic and speeches that could undermine India's sovereignty were something that was to be solved. Hence, security of the state as an exception was preferred over sedition as an exception to tackle those turbulent times.

1. History of Hate Speech in India

In India, two communitics have been in conflict with each other, the Hindus and the Muslims. This is one of the reasons that India after gaining Independence chose to be a secular state so that all the communities that have been residing in India since ages continue to live together in harmony and enshrine the spirit of brotherhood. Before independence, there have been countless instances of brotherhood and also of conflict amongst the two communities. Controversial material relating to religious supremacy of one over the other religion or religious rebuking has been the cause of this conflict. Hate speech laws were the need of the hour and provisions for tackling this problem were made in the IPC.

Historically, hate speech was itself an element for the offence of sedition in England. But the draft prepared by Macaulay did not contain such element within the ambit of sedition. Even Stephen did not include hate speech in the 1870 amendment to IPC under section 124A. It was in the year 1898; a new provision was in itself inserted into IPC as section 153A to deal with the problem of hate speech rather than amending the provision of sedition. Thus hate speech was made a criminal offence, as it was necessary in a country like India where there are diversities on the lines religion, race, caste and community.[22]

One of the most prominent instances involving hate speech is Lekh Ram incident in the year 1897 at Lahore. The deceased belonged to the Arya Samaj community. He wrote a brochure criticising Islam as a religion in a harsh and demeaning manner in the year 1892 and in the following year, Mirza Ahmad, the founder of Ahmadiya sect made a prophecy that Lekh ram would die in the coming six years as a result of his brochure that criticised Islam. In 1897, Lekh Ram was murdered and in the following year, section tackling hate speech was inserted into the IPC. This incident along with incidents of cow killings and other incidents taking place in other parts of the country justified the need for insertion of the provision.[23]

While most of the members of the Viceroy's Council found insertion if this provision favourable, some of the other members which consisted of mostly Indians, dissented. The Indians found this provision to be an obstruction to social reforms that were needed at that time. Reforms such as vegetarianism, widow re-marriage, Prarthana Samaj and anti idol movement would be obstructed as speaking against any religion or its form would attract the provisions of section 153A. While one of the member, Chitnavis found that there was no need for such provision as both the communities have for long lived in peace and harmony and only recent instances of communal discord have necessitated such provision. Furthermore, in cases of all of a sudden religious discord cannot be solved by such hate speech laws. This provision only came into being in the year 1926.[24]

In *P.K. Chakravarty v. Emperor*[25], a bench of two judges of Calcutta High Court decided the case concerning a daily called '*Forward*' which called out the Muslims to carry out violence amongst themselves. It was held that the intent of the publisher has to be seen and not the context of the article. In newspapers, it is seen that reporting might be done mentioning killing of a person belonging to a particular community by a person who belongs to other community. This does not necessarily violate provisions of section 153A. The judgement declared that this particular article did not violate the provision dealing with class hatred.

The following year, one of the most highlighted cases of class hatred took place. It was the *Rangila Rasul*[26] case. The title meant 'colourful prophet', being very provocative, was the work by Pandit Champauti, an Arya Samaji. The said article in the form of a pamphlet was published in the year 1924 and was decided by a judge of Lahore High court. Justice Dalip Singh, who was a non-muslim, held that the article was a religious satire on the Prophet but it however showed nothing that was attacking Muslim religion. Although he accepted that it was written with malicious intent and could harm religious cord between the communities, he opined that the said provision invoked in this case was meant to prevent or tackle people from hurting each other on religious lines and not for critics to stop attacking deceased religious leaders. Even though such material could be scurrilous and bad in nature but if such cases are brought within the ambit of section 153A, all the historic works could be questioned, which was not the purpose of the insertion of this provision.

There was hue and cry in the North West Frontier Provinces of British India as this judgment received heavy criticism. However, a daily named '*Muslim Outlook*' carried a piece mentioning that the judge received some considerations for the judgment. This piece was held for contempt of court. This case was followed by another case, *Devi Sharan*. Devi Sharan was sentenced to rigorous imprisonment of one year for authoring an article, 'Sair-i-Dozakh' which mean a trip to hell. He in this article mentions himself in a dream on trip to heaven and hell, where in hell he sees the Prophet suffering. The case was decided by judges, Broadway and Skcmp, both Britishers and found the article to be hurtful to sentiments of one community and hence attracted elements of section 153A.[27]

In 1927, an amendment was moved for amending IPC and section 295-A was inserted making it an offence if the person deliberately coupled with malicious intention outrages the religious feelings of others or insults the religious belief of a person or religion as a whole. This section became a matter of huge debate in the Legislative Council as members namely; A. Rangaswami Iyenagar, Arthur Moore, K.C. Roy, N.C. Chander and N.C. Kelkar insisted that insertion of such provision would hamper various social reforms being carried on. Furthermore, those who believed in the evolution of traditional beliefs into the modern practices thought such provisions would curb their reformatory work even though they wanted to do so keeping in conformity the former practices. It was Jinnah who felt this provision was carrying with it enough punishment and it was because of him that the offence was made non-bailable.[28]

4. Hate Speech and Sedition Law: The Conflict

Freedom of Speech and Expression is not as simple as it appears. It attracts great attention from all nooks and corner of the society and also a greater criticism. People in the guise of their right to speech and expression go without holding back and without any respect for law expressing ideas that sometimes vitiate basic human values. Right to choice: to marry, to choose one's gender, to reside throughout India, to choose clothes as one likes and so on. These basic choices that are intrinsic in human beings become a point of discrimination from a set of people who feel themselves more superior to others.

Hate Speech goes at the root of race superiority and extends to more than just religion. Anti-gay speeches and speeches that target minorities based on the basis of race, caste or religion are something that has been rampant and on the rise as the society is growing and expanding its horizons.

[1] CAD, Vol. XI, p.616 (17 November 1949).

[2] Abhinav Chandrachud, RHETORIC OF REPUBLIC: FREE SPEECH AND THE CONSTITUTION OF INDIA, Penguin Books (2017), p. 20.

[3] *Queen Empress v. Bal Gangadhar Tilak* (1897) ILR 22 Bom 112.

[4] *Id.*, at pp. 24-25.

[5] Shivani Lohiya, LAW OF SEDITION, Universal Law Publishing Co. (2014), p. 2.

[6] *Ibid.*

[7]*Queen Empress v. Jogendra Chandra Bose* (1891) ILR 19 Cal 35.

[8] Abhinav Chandrachud, RHETORIC OF REPUBLIC: FREE SPEECH AND THE CONSTITUTION OF INDIA, Penguin Books (2017), p. 28.

[9] *Ibid.*

[10] *Queen Empress v. Bal Gangadhar Tilak* (1897) ILR 22 Bom 112.

[11] Abhinav Chandrachud, RHETORIC OF REPUBLIC: FREE SPEECH AND THE CONSTITUTION OF INDIA, Penguin Books (2017), pp. 31-33.

[12] *Queen Empress v. Ramchandra Narayan* (1897) 22 ILR Bom 152 (FB).

[13] *Queen Empress v. Amba Prasad* (1898) ILR 20 All 55.

[14] Shivani Lohiya, LAW OF SEDITION, Universal Law Publishing Co. (2014), pp. 3-6.

[15] Munshi's draft, Article V (1) and (2). Select Documents II, p. 75.

[16] Ambedkar's draft, Article II (1), (12) and (7). Select Documents II, 4(ii) (d), pp. 86-7.

[17] Section 153A "*Promoting enmity between different groups on ground of religion, race, place of birth, residence, language, etc., and doing acts prejudicial to maintenance of harmony*"—(1) Whoever— (a) by words, either spoken or written, or by signs or by visible representations or otherwise, promotes or attempts to promote, on grounds of religion, race, place of birth, residence, language, caste or community or any other ground whatsoever, disharmony or feelings of enmity, hatred or ill will between different religious, racial, language or regional groups or castes or communities, or

(b) commits any act which is prejudicial to the maintenance of harmony between different religious, racial, language or regional groups or castes or communities, and which disturbs or is likely to disturb the public tranquillity, or

(c) organizes any exercise, movement, drill or other similar activity intending that the participants in such activity shall use or be trained to use criminal force or violence or knowing it to be likely that the participants in such activity will use or be trained to use criminal force or violence, or participates in such activity intending to use or be trained to use criminal force or violence or knowing it to be likely that the participants in such activity will use or be trained to use criminal force or violence, against any religious, racial, language or regional group or caste or community and such activity for any reason whatsoever causes or is likely to cause fear or alarm or a feeling of insecurity amongst members of such religious, racial, language or regional group or caste or community, shall be punished with imprisonment which may extend to three years, or with fine, or with both.

[18] B Shiva Rao, FRAMING OF INDIA'S CONSTITUTION, N.M. Tripathi Pvt. Ltd. (1968), p. 212.

[19] *Ibid.*

[20] *Id.*, at p. 215.

[21] CAD, Vol.7, pp. 735-762.

[22] Abhinav Chandrachud, RHETORIC OF REPUBLIC: FREE SPEECH AND THE CONSTITUTION OF INDIA, Penguin Books (2017), p. 226.

[23] *Ibid.*

[24] *Ibid.*

[25] AIR 1926 Cal 1133.

[26] *Raj Paul v. Emperor*, AIR 1927 Lah 590.

[27] Shivani Lohiya, LAW OF SEDITION, Universal Law Publishing Co. (2014), p. 22.

[28] 295A "*Deliberate and malicious acts, intended to outrage religious feelings of any class by insulting its religion or religious beliefs*"—Whoever, with deliberate and malicious intention of outraging the religious feelings of any class of citizens of India, by words, either spoken or written, or by signs or by visible representations or otherwise, insults or attempts to insult the religion or the religious beliefs of that class, shall be punished with imprisonment of either description for a term which may extend to three years, or with fine, or with both.

CHAPTER TWO

JURISPRUDENTIAL AND INTERNATION SCENARIO ON HATE SPEECH

2.1 Introductory

This chapter deals with the jurisprudential approach with regard to freedom of speech and expression. Contemporary view of jurists along with modern views of some authors has also been incorporated in this chapter. Moving ahead, international framework comprising of various conventions has been deal with along with the inclusion of global perspective of hate speech. Hate Speech effects includes totalitarianism, negationism, homophobia and other spheres have been dealt by involving case laws. In respect of Global perspective, South Africa, Canada and United States of America are included to showcase the present status of free speech and expression and how global players tackle the menace of hate speech.

2.2 Freedom of Speech and Expression: Jurisprudential Approach

Free Speech is a right that is intrinsic to every human being and just like every issue it attracts at least two approaches. One approach advocates about absolute free speech and sees restrictions as curbing the growth of a democracy. The second approach deals with enjoyment of this right but advocates for regulation of speech. Dworkin, Robert Post, Jack Balkin and Justice Holmes are the chief proponents of the first approach while John Stuart Mill, John Locke and Jeremy Waldron advocate for the second approach.

1. *First View: Absolute Freedom of Speech*

ii. **Ronald Dworkin:** He was a staunch supporter of absolute free speech and brought forth the importance of free speech as a leading factor in growth for a democracy. He said that in a democracy one cannot have the right to be not insulted or the least, offended. The rationale behind this approach is that criticism is the most important factor in progress of a society and ultimately the country. Therefore, insulating oneself from criticism on the pretext of dignity and contempt is something that Dworkin has negated as an argument against Hate Speech.[1]

It is for him a compromise which is made so as to reap the benefits of a democracy. Criticism or ridicule towards one sect or religion has to be crafted as per the democracy. Such criticism cannot be toned down and presented as a lesser version of the original criticism as it could lead to something which was not intended in first place. Criticism has been since the advent of democracy an important tool for various noble political movements. Free Speech is a price which the citizens of a democracy have to pay.[2]

ii. **Robert Post:** Post comes in when Dworkin fails. Dworkin has presented something that is farfetched and it may ultimately fail to achieve its objective. Robert Post has mentioned democracy as a notion of self determination and presents citizens as the regulator for political autonomy. He was against any regulation of free speech and forecasted that citizens ought to be the ultimate or the sole regulator for political sovereignty. Thus free speech without any sort of regulations was his choice irrespective of the outcome of such speech.[3]

iii. **Jack Balkin:** He is known as the champion of free speech and stresses upon the need for free speech as an exemplary tool for democratic culture in a society. His theory is founded upon three essential features that are essential for free speech. These are firstly, Interactivity, secondly it is mass participation and lastly it is the capability to bring forth transform or modification in the existing culture.[4]

He tries to distinguish between free speech as a right in a democracy and a republic. Democracy provides ample room for individual and their ideas while republic regime diminishes the importance of non-political expression and individual liberty. For Balkin, an ideal democratic culture would be where an individual can come forward and participate actively in decision making process, hence democratic deliberation.[5]

iv. **Justice Holmes:** Holmes's theory provides a very restrictive look on the first instance but when carefully read it produces a different image. The confusion arose because of the judgment of *Abrams v. United States*[6], which appears to impose restrictions upon free speech but when one delves deep into it produces a different image. Human beings have different opinions about various events and therefore produce an emotional and subjective response to the speech. The speech that is different to our opinion or poses obstacle to our pre conceived notions is the one that we dislike and hate.[7]

Thus, according to Holmes, restrictions are necessary if such speech causes clear and present danger. On the issue of group hatred, he advocates that these groups should enjoy freedom of speech and make the world according as they please.

2. *Second view: Regulated Freedom of Speech*

i. **John Stuart Mill:** Mill's view resonates with Bentham's theory of Pleasure and Pain. He further adds that free speech is essential to the development of mental well being of mankind. But with this right there comes a caveat attached to it. If one is exercising the right to speech and expression then such person should exercise so keeping in mind that such speech should no cause pain to others.[8]

An act which provides happiness in the longer run is placed on a higher pedestal than an act which is concerned with limited present needs. This pretext is based on the basis that happiness of human being is greater than that of a beast as the former is nobler than the latter.[9]

ii. **John Locke:** He supported restrictions upon free speech and held that individual's act or an independent act should not harm other beings well being. It should not be detrimental to other's life, liberty or possessions, the three inalienable rights which cannot be compromised. Restrictions can be placed upon these three rights if the masses and their well being is in concern and rights of the masses can be ensured through such restrictions. Such restrictions should be reasonable and hence backed by statutory provisions and are not to be imposed in an arbitrary manner.[10]

iii. **Jeremy Waldron:** Waldron is a professor of law at the New York University and is one of the chief proponents of the hate speech issue in the 21st century. Waldron focuses on the issue of hate speech when it becomes discriminatory especially towards a minority. In his book '*The Harm in Hate Speech*' he has mentioned about Islamophobia and how it has caused feared in the Islamic community who are living in a civilised society.[11]

Dependence on free speech is just like one depends on clean and fresh air. The things that defy our surrounding environment should be a cause of concern of law. Hate speech not only causes society to be at stake but also the legal sphere also gets entangled along with this menace. It is at stake in two ways. Firstly, the inclusiveness of all members of society is an important factor for constituting public good and the social norms make such commitment inevitable. Secondly, there exists a sense of security in a given society which also forms the basis of such society. Hate Speech undermines these vital postulates.[12]

Hate speech in some way causes the past incidents of violence to reoccur and pose threat to social peace in a peaceful environment of social order. It is also to be seen from the vision of those who have certain assurances from the community they are living in are put in question due to hate speech. The assurance to live in a dignified manner along with right to a peaceful environment is all put in jeopardy. The dignity of any minority community is put in danger and publication of any form of hate speech undermines the above mentioned assurances.[13]

Jeremy Waldron has mentioned in his book about the 'Well ordered society' concept of John Rawls. Rawls in his work '*Political Liberalism*' has mentioned about a social order that is the basic structure of a civilised society. This structure is regulated by the novel principles of justice and the growing needs of the people. According to Waldron, it is this basic structure that is violated by signs or posters published that attack the dignity and the ethnicity of certain class of people. In the end, it is the social harm that is posed due to unregulated free speech and causes substantive harm to a legislature that aims to suppress such violations through their laws.[14]

2.3 International Scenario on Hate Speech

2.3.1 The Conflict between Hate Speech Regulations and Fundamental Freedoms

There is no doubt that each and every set of society or community tends to show variation in each and every manner. Their lifestyle and religious practices vary and it becomes necessary that differences aside, there is reconciliation between the right to freedom of thought and expression with the right to practice religion and the right to be protected from any form of discrimination. Sometimes, when there are attempts of amalgamation of these rights, there is friction in the society as these rights touch every person living in the societies.[15]

ECHR or the European Court of Human Rights (ECHR) guarantees right to freedom of expression under Article 10[16] of the Convention. Right to freedom of thought is an absolute right while the same absolution is not bestowed upon the right to freedom of expression. This right as pointed in clause 2 of the said article mentions about duties and responsibilities that have been casted upon the persons who exercise this right and furthermore, mention that such exercise has to be in accordance with the law. Thus *forum externum* (freedom of expression) not bestowed with such guaranteed exercise like *forum internum* (freedom of thought) has been bestowed with. It has been observed by the court that: “it is particularly conscious of the vital importance of combating racial discrimination in all its forms and manifestations”, thereby understanding its pivotal role in the fight against racism and other forms of discrimination.[17]

The court has observed in the *Gunduz*[18] judgment:

“that tolerance and respect for the equal dignity of all human beings constitute the foundations of a democratic, pluralistic society. That being so, as a matter of principle it may be considered necessary in certain democratic societies to sanction or even prevent all forms of expression which spread, incite, promote or justify hatred based on intolerance (including religious intolerance), provided that any “formalities”, “conditions”, “restrictions” or “penalties” imposed are proportionate to the legitimate aim pursued”.

The authorities must strive to work out an equitable basis on which the interests of the diverse communities and their rights can both be worked out in a peaceful manner.

2.3.2 The Concept of Hate Speech

There has been considerable usage of the term hate speech although it has not been specifically defined anywhere yet. Numbers of States across the globe have adopted hate speech legislations that prescribe the scope of elements that have been labelled as hate speech. It is the recommendation (97) sub-clause 20 of the Council of Europe's Committee that defines hate speech as:

"the term hate speech shall be understood as covering all forms of expression which spread, incite, promote or justify racial hatred, xenophobia, anti-Semitism or other forms of hatred based on intolerance, including: intolerance expressed by aggressive nationalism and ethnocentrism, discrimination and hostility against minorities, migrants and people of immigrant origin".[19]

Although European courts have not followed a singular definition, they have described hate speech as an offence based on the lines of intolerance and expression that tend to incite hatred amongst communities. The court does not limit itself by the definitions given across the globe by various courts with regard to hate speech. Hate speech is not an isolated topic but contains multitude of events that result into it. It includes three basic elements, firstly hate in the form of words or any other form of expression towards a particular race; secondly, provocation of violence into the minds of people on the basis of religion and thirdly, it based on extreme nationalism and ethnicity. Gay rights movements have seen widespread criticism from traditionalists and hence, homophobic speech also falls within the ambit of hate speech.[20]

Therefore, there arises an important question as to identification of hate speech as sometimes speeches may appear to be rational at first but in the guise of rationality, hatred might be manifested to the listeners. Thus, strict adherence to certain postulates such as judicial precedents and covenants that make hate speech not only identifiable but also prosecution worthy across the globe should be complied with.

2.4 International Treaties and Conventions

2.4.1 European Council

Article 11[21] of the Council of Europe happens to be the most prominent provision that establishes freedom of expression as one of the essential values to human right. But there are other conventions, whether binding or non-binding they are promising from the viewpoint of human rights. State that are signatory to such conventions are expected to provide the minorities of their country to be at the same footing as the majority are. Eliminating discrimination is the one of the most basic duty of a modern state in 21st century.

However, there is a convention on Cybercrime that prohibit dissemination of hateful information and messages through the medium of Internet. Xenophobia is the propagation of ideas that promote hatred towards a particular nation. The messages that promote xenophobic approach or at times racist content are to be held as criminally liable offences under the domestic laws of various signatory countries. Furthermore, messages that justify genocide in any part of the world should constitute hate speech and person transmitting such information should be held liable.[22]

Council of Europe: Although the council can resort to the existing treaties, it also drafts recommendations through which the Minister's council drafts regulations for its various parties. These are of non-binding nature but they act as guiding principles in eliminating discrimination of any form.[23] Following are the observations:

"Recommendation (97)20 is based on eliminating hate speech and takes into its ambit any form of hatred such as hatred based on race, xenophobic approach or anti Jews views. Adopted on 30th October 1997, it condemns the above mentioned forms of hate speech and casts the liability on the maker of such hate speech as well as responsibility on the media to promote such news that serves public interest".[24]

"Recommendation 1805(2007) is a recommendation for acting against insults based on religion and hate speeches on the basis of religion which was adopted on 29th June, 2007. The parliamentary assembly prescribes penalising such acts of hate speech that promote hatred or insults that target people on the ground of their religion. It also casts responsibility on the States to make provisions for tackling such menace under their domestic law".[25]

2.4.2 United Nations

Although International Covenants have existed, the Human Rights Committee (HRC) under the aegis of United Nations has made certain recommendation that validate various conventions. The most prominent out of these recommendations are those based upon Article 19, 20 of the International Covenant on Civil and Political Rights (ICCPR) and Article 4 of the Elimination of all forms of racial discrimination.

General Comment No. 10: The HRC stated the following with regard to Article 19[26] that deals with freedom of expression as follows:

"Paragraph 3 expressly stresses that the exercise of the right to freedom of expression carries with it special duties and responsibilities and for this reason certain restrictions on the right are permitted which may relate either to the interests of other persons or to those of the community as a whole".[27]

Establishing nexus between Article 19 and 20 of the covenant, the HRC took note of various war propagandas that exists throughout the world and the xenophobic approach that has caused hatred amongst people of different nations and mentioned the following:

"Article 20 of the Covenant states that any propaganda for war and any advocacy of national, racial or religious hatred that constitutes incitement to discrimination, hostility or violence shall be prohibited by law. In the opinion of the Committee, these required prohibitions are fully compatible with the right of freedom of expression as contained in article 19, the exercise of which carries with it special duties and responsibilities. The prohibition under paragraph 1 extends to all forms of propaganda threatening or resulting in an act of aggression or breach of the peace contrary to the Charter of the United Nations, while paragraph 2 is directed against any advocacy of national, racial or religious hatred that constitutes incitement to discrimination, hostility or violence, whether such propaganda or advocacy has aims which are internal or external to the State concerned. For article 20 to become fully effective there ought to be a law making it clear that propaganda and advocacy as described therein are contrary to public policy and providing for an appropriate sanction in case of violation".[28]

While the Committee on elimination of racial discrimination presented its report and recommended that the states should strive more hard to tackle the problems related to hatred spread due to hate speeches that promote racial discrimination and xenophobic ideas. It also mentioned to eliminate such targets that are mostly targeted on the lines of their minority status and the stigmatization that follows these attacks should be looked into and eliminated.[29]

2.4.3 Hate Speech vis-a-vis International Covenant on Civil and Political Rights

Article 19 and 20 of the International Covenant on Civil and Political Rights (ICCPR) specifically deals with the issue of freedom of speech and expression and hate speech. While article 19 deals with the guarantee of freedom of speech and expression, article 20 on the other hands specifically deals with the problem of hatred in the society. Any advocacy of hatred is prohibited as per the provisions of article 20. Therefore, it deems fit that Article 19 and 20 be read together to deal with the issue of hate speech and freedom of speech.[30]

Article 19 brings with itself certain tests that are required for adjudging restrictions that are necessary for regulation of speech in a modern setup. The method to adjudge involves a three step test. Firstly, in order a restriction is imposed, it should be in accordance with the law that is specifically provided in a statue or law. Secondly, such restriction must be imposed to tackle the issue of public order and morality. Also, if the state is imposing such restriction it can do so in the case of national security or friendly relations with other states. Lastly, the state should show that the restrictions imposed are the minimal steps taken for achieving goals that are proportionate to such limitations.[31]

Article 20 deals with the issue of propagation of hate on the lines of extreme nationalism. It mentions that it is prohibited for people to insist upon advocacy of war and any acts of aggression. Dealing with the issue of Xenophobia, it specifically bars any such action if such speeches propagating hatred or acts of aggressions lead to incitement of violence or hate or the worst discrimination in the community. The act of spreading hatred alone is not held to violative of this article but it the incitement or the provocation it brings with itself that is held as violative.[32]

In 1996, a case *Robert Faurisson v. France*[33] came up in France that dealt with the violation of article 20. In this case, a professor was following the negation method and hence, denied any acts of genocide and Nazi holocaust in the class filled with students. He defended himself by saying that such act of anti-semitism is restricting his fundamental freedom of speech and historical research. But it was held that this act was consistent with the laws in France and was violative of the principle enshrined in the covenant.

2.4.4 Universal Declaration of Human Rights

Article 7[34] of the UDHR guarantees equality to all human beings in the form of their right against discrimination along with any provocation to discrimination is held to violative of this principle.

Article 29[35] of the UDHR allows certain restrictions to be cast upon various freedom and rights so as to maintain peace and tranquillity. Furthermore, issues of morality and public order vary from place to place and hence, certain restrictions that are reasonable can be imposed in accordance with law. Lastly it has been more specifically mentioned that restrictions cannot go against the principles of the United Nations.

2.5 Judicial Assessment of Hate Speech

The Courts have devised three tests that it follows while it contemplates whether a speech adds up to hate speech or not. When it has been set up that there has been impedance with freedom of expression, the courts resort to a three-step investigation to decide the Constitutionality of such obstruction. These restrictions should be reasonable and should be backed by law.[36]

i. Whether the restriction imposed is backed by law?

The law that permits the restriction upon article 10 of ECHR must be recommended by some statute. It must be followed true to its letter so that the citizens can regularise their conduct as per the restrictions imposed upon. This has to be observed so that the consequences arising out of such impositions can be foreseen and conduct regularised in accordance with law.[37]

ii. Whether there is a nexus between the restrictions imposed and the object sought to be achieved?

The restrictions cast upon the freedom of speech should be in consonance with the problem sought to be weeded out. The reason for which such the right is curtailed should be reasonable as has been held in the *Handyside*[38] judgment. If such restriction does not mitigate the problem, then it can be challenged in the court of law and the judges can decide upon the same keeping in mind the circumstance and facts of the case.

iii. Whether such restrictions are needed in a modern democratic setup?

Every Constitution and every covenant have some values enshrined that continue to guide the legislators across the globe. These pious values should be kept in mind while imposing restrictions upon such inviolable and intrinsic fundamental freedoms that form the backbone of a modern democratic society. Furthermore, it has to be seen that the speech so curtailed is done so after following all the investigative methods as all the speech have been kept on the same pedestal. This approach extends the liberal and Dworkin's view about free speech.

As mentioned above where all the speeches are treated on the same footing is something that ECHR has done away with recently. The rationale behind imposition of restrictions is to be judged on two levels. First, it has to be investigated whether such restriction imposed was required or not. Second and most importantly, whether such action is permissible in a modern democratic setup or not.[39]

Apart from the above mentioned point, it is further observed that in a society where diverse communities exist, free speech leads to violation of anti-discrimination policies which upset not only minorities but also the ethos that have prevailed in a peaceful society.[40]

Putting all kinds of speeches, offensive and legitimate one's on the same footing is violative of the equality principle: "equals amongst equals". The Union has strived to strike a balance between these two composites of society. The ECHR has not defined 'hate speech' but has made shift in its approach of keeping all kinds of speeches on an equal footing to an approach where speeches are to judged in the manner they are made. This leads to the point that 'Hate Speech' is not protected by Article 10 of the covenant, thereby shifting the burden of establishing the elements of hate speech on the judiciary.[41] It is observed that hate speech causes certain effects in a society, which is discussed in the following sub part.

2.6 Effects of Hate Speech

Hate Speech brings with itself wide amplitudes of problems. It ranges from corrupting people's mind by speaking on totalitarianism and negationism. Furthermore, speeches that attack on the grounds of race and sexuality are something that poses great problem for the State across the globe. Internet has been the medium of communication that has surpassed all the mediums in recent years. Through internet, messages are communicated equivocating for thoughts mentioned above, thus information is disseminated at speed unprecedented for. Following are the effects of hate speech and further mentions the judicial interpretation of problems posed so far.

2.6.1 Hate Speech and Totalitarianism

Society's progress and so do the political philosophy along side. In Europe, the revival of socialism was seen and the democratic order was being challenged through the measures of totalitarianism. Such political ideology was held as being contrary to the provisions of the convention and article 17 of the European Convention had to be casted upon. The court in the case of *Communist Party (KPD) v. the Federal Republic of German*[42] held that such ideology is not in consonance with the democratic principles and are against human rights. Article 17 mentions that the provisions of the convention do not in any way empower the states to strike upon the fundamental freedoms of the citizens from more than that is held as permissible according to the convention. Basically, no state or even person can go beyond the reasonable restrictions and cast such impositions that violate the human rights.[43]

In the above mentioned case, communist ideology was being spread by utilising the mass movement underway and paved way for dictatorship. It was the time of cold war and such act would have impaired the government in power to deal with widespread atrocities. Thus activities that in the guise of mass movements spread socialism would be contrary to the convention.[44]

2.6.2 Hate Speech and Negationism

Negationism is a derivate of the word negation. It means to refuse to particular event, mostly historical. Free speech has been violated at many instances whereby heinous crimes such the genocide of Jews: the Holocaust has been held to be not ever occurred and deny any such crime. Such speech has been held to be violative as it equivocates the Anti-Semitism views.

There is a rise in the speakers that not only condone the acts of genocide but even pacify with such acts.[45]

In the case of *Honsik v. Austria*[46], the commission arrived at the decision that the views expressed in the published book propagates the idea that the holocaust never occurred and that there was no organised mass killings of Jews. These statements were held to violative of the basic essentials of peace and tranquillity and promote racial discrimination.[47]

Furthermore, any remarks that are made against the ideals enshrined in the covenant and those which promote views that are in favour of Nazi's are held to be against the Article 10 and 17, as has been held in the case of *Lehideux*[48]. The court in this case held that any views that promote Anti-Semitism or any form of racism are against the covenant itself holding covenant as fundamental in upholding human rights. Denial of heinous acts is denial of the basic values casted in the covenant.

2.6.3 Hate Speech and Racism

Other than revision of historical events, the European court used Article 17 as a means to nudge the attempts of racial discrimination that was beyond the scope of negationism and constituted racial hate speech. In *Glimmerveen*[49] case, the court went on to use article 17 as a means to nudge the argument that article 10 saved the speech in question. The document unmistakably included components of racial separation and hence couldn't depend entirely upon Article 10. For this situation, the applicants had been indicted for having flyers routed to "White Dutch people", which would in general ensure that each one that was not white left the Netherlands.

In another prominent case namely, *Jersild*[50], that dealt with racial hate speech, the court held that people who belonged to the group called 'Greenjackets' were convicted and their act of racial hate speech was not protected under article 10 of the covenant.

In first of its case, the court applied article 17 in the attack that was aimed at persons belonging to Muslim religion. This was the *Norwood*[51] case, wherein the appellant had hung out a poster on his house's window that depicted the event of 9/11 September attacks and mentioned that Islam, (depicted by their religious symbol of crescent moon and a star) should step out of British soil. The court explained that this was stereotyping a religion and attributing an act of terrorism and linking it to a religion is beyond any saving of article 10 and held it to be violative of article 17.[52]

2.6.4 Hate Speech and Sexual Orientation

Homophobic comments mean rebuking people on the basis of their sexuality. People have been since time immemorial known to be homosexual in their sexuality. They have been rebuked for having such sexuality and are often subject to discrimination due to their sexuality. The court has held that any remarks that promote such phobias are to be not protected as free speech as this goes against the human values of right to choose their sex.[53]

The Swedish Supreme Court had held the pamphlets that carried offensive ideas and comments with regard to LGBT community were bad in law. The comments in this particular case were held to be oppressive and though the idea to express oneself is protected under hate speech but making offensive statements about one's sexuality and their gender choice goes against the human value of not offending others. Even transgender are subject to immense discrimination because of their appearance and sexuality and hence such comments that target them and their community are held as hate speech. The Swedish court had paved the way for such speeches to be bad in law and the same was re-iterated by the European court in the *Vejdeland*[54] case.

2.7 International Scenario

2.7.1 South Africa

The right to freedom of speech and expression has been Constitutional status in the South African Constitution. Although there is not absolute freedom of expression as it is regulated by reasonable restrictions. Such provision is contained in Section 16 of the South African Constitution and the reasonable restrictions are mentioned under sub-clause (2) of the aforesaid section. Hate Speech finds mention in the South African Constitution specifically as a restriction upon free speech and hence is not protected speech. Restrictions such as incitement to violence, promoting acts of aggression in the form of war or propagating hatred on the basis of race, religion, gender or ethnicity that are likely to cause violence have been cast upon as restriction upon the freedom of expression.[55]

Hate speech is not limited to just mass programmes and events but exists at workplaces too. Working class is subject to discrimination based on race, religion and ethnicity. In one of such cases, Nomasomi, a worker was subject to hate speech and for such inhuman treatment got awarded damages. The South African court of equality awarded such damages based on section 10 of the Prevention of Unfair Discrimination Act. This provision specifically disallows people from carrying out acts that are hurtful or likely to be hurtful or promote hatred via any medium of communication. Advocating or propagation of any of discriminatory ideas is held to be liable under law.[56]

2.7.2 Canada

There are domestic laws that influenced by various international human rights based conventions. Canada also has incorporated these fundamental rights in the form of Canadian Charter of Rights and Freedoms. Section 2 of the said charter promotes freedom of thought, expression, belief and opinion. Furthermore, this provision is also not absolute and entails restrictions upon these above mentioned rights. Apart from this charter, the procedural laws in Canada such as the Criminal Code of Canada also take into its ambit the hatred that is spread in public domain and its propagation.

There is ample amount of judicial involvement into the issue of hate speech in Canada. The Supreme Court of Canada has in the case of *Keegstra*[57] held as follows:

"Parliament has recognized the substantial harm that can flow from hate propaganda and, in trying to prevent the pain suffered by target group members and to reduce racial, ethnic and religious tension and perhaps even violence in Canada, has decided to suppress the wilful promotion of hatred against identifiable groups. Parliament's objective is supported not only by the work of numerous study groups, but also by our collective historical knowledge of the potentially catastrophic effects of the promotion of hatred. Additionally, the international commitment to eradicate hate propaganda and Canada's commitment to the values of equality and multiculturalism in ss. 15 and 27 of the Charter strongly buttresses the importance of this objective".[58]

Tests devised to verify restrictions imposed upon freedom of expression. The Canadian judiciary has devised certain rules that need to be followed before imposing restrictions upon freedom of speech. Without observation of these rules, the restrictions imposed upon can be struck down as bad in law. At few other instances, the court laid down the procedural requirements which were re-iterated in *Keegstra*[59] case. The Following rules need to be followed:

i. The restrictions that are imposed should have a connection with the problem that has been sought to be weeded out.
ii. The problem that has been posed to be removed should be done by imposing restrictions in a toned down manner so that the freedom of expression is curtailed as least as possible.
iii. The measures taken for restricting freedoms of the citizens must be in the same proportion as the problem posed.[60]

Another significant judicial pronouncement has successfully laid down the postulates that determine the offence of hate speech in Canada. There are three methods by which speech can be adjudged whether it constitutes hate speech or not. This was laid down in the year 2013 in the case of *Saskatchewan (Human Rights Commission) v. Whatcott*[61]. The first test is the determination of any speech in an impartial manner from the view point of an ordinary prudent man and whether it falls under the scope of hate speech or not. The second test is that the enactments that deal with the issue of hate speech have to be seen in an intense manner such that it could not possibly leave an iota of doubt over the matter in hand. Lastly and most importantly, cases involving hate speech and the alleged hate material should be decided by the Court.[62]

Apart from hate speech, the Canadian law has gone a step further and brought into its ambit such content that is false and has the possibility of creating any public disorder. Information or news that is false or the person publicising such news knows that such information is not true has the probability of causing harm to the interests of the society. Such material should be prevented from being spread so as to maintain the unity in a diverse country such as Canada that houses people from across the world. Also views that support anti Jew teachings or statements tend to vitiate the ethos of social and educational institutions.[63]

2.7.3 United States of America

Hate Speech in the United States goes back to the year 1952, wherein the conflict of race was at its peak. The problem of whites and blacks go back centuries from present day as slavery created a division between the people of America. Joseph Beauharnais belonged to a White circle league of America which was a white supremacist group. He was the leader of this group and with the help of its other members, dispensed pamphlets that had called upon the Mayor of Chicago and the City council to stop the encroachment upon the property of white people by the blacks or 'Negro'. He was agitated over the issue of blacks being involved in a number of criminal activities and provoked the fellow Americans by saying that if by the method of these persuasions they do not join the cause, the criminal acts such robberies, rape and other such heinous crimes would in near future.[64]

In Illinois, there was a provision by which any act that depicts a community or a group of people on the basis of their race, colour or ethnicity as criminals or in a derogatory manner to be held as an offence. This statue was challenged in the Supreme Court which held this provision to be constitutionally valid by a majority of 5-4.[65]

This decision in present times does not hold out to be a good decision as this was not followed in the case of *Village of Skokie*[66] case in the year 2011. The members of the Nationalist Socialist Party of America were supporters of the Nazi regime and wanted to organise an event in the Skokie village of Illinois. The village had nearly seventy thousand occupants and in majority consisted of followers of Jewish religion and a also a large part of them were the surviving members of the Nazi torture. The members of the march were supposed to be dressed in the uniforms that would depict Swastika symbols on the uniforms in the form of armbands or emblems.[67]

The members of the Jewish community approached the court to get an injunction issued in order to be not subject to such event. The Supreme Court of Illinois refused to grant an injunction as the information of the march that was supposed to take place was given in advance. Prior information acts as a defence for the persons carrying out events that otherwise maybe hurtful to a particular community. Such act was allowed as the members who did not wish this event to take place could simply not attend such event.[68]

Educational institutions happen to be a breeding ground for diverse ideologies. During propagation and dissemination of their political ideologies or ideas may lead to acts that could constitute the offence of hate speech. Therefore, many institutions and colleges started enacting rules and regulations that prohibited hate speech on their premises. One of the examples of such regulations happen to be of the Stanford University wherein in the year 1990, speeches that would end up discriminating or stigmatizing any minority group or any class of people based on their race, colour or ethnicity or for that matter even their sexuality were not permitted. However, this regulation in the case of *Robert J. Corry v. Stanford University*[69] was struck down by the Court of California state.

One of the leading cases of hate speeches in the United States is *R.A.V. v. City of St. Paul*[70].In the town of Minnesota there was a provision for the offence of misdemeanour that held people liable if they planted things or objects that would otherwise be hurtful to the sentiments of any particular community based on the grounds of race, gender, ethnicity, religion or colour. In the present case, the petitioners had planted a cross in the lawn of a Negro family that were occupants of the house across their house. They wanted to convey to that black family that they were not welcome in their surroundings and did not want them as their neighbours. These miscreants would have been framed under the offence of trespass or any other offences but instead were charged under the previously mentioned misdemeanour.

This provision was challenged in the court and Justice Scalia delivered the majority judgment. It was held by the court that such provision only catered the vilification of one form of speech and was limited in scope. On this basis the court struck down thus provision for discerning between different standpoints.[71]

In another case where a funeral service was being held for Matthew Synder, a member of American armed forces who was killed in Iraq war, a case of hate speech was witnessed. The funeral service was organised by the deceased's father and during this service, a Baptist Church of Westboro had gathered around the service area and were protesting with signs such as 'Soldier was not a homosexual', 'Priests Rape Boys', 'Thank God for IED's', 'You're going to hell', etc. The martyred soldier's father sued the Church for such discriminatory and hatred filled remarks and was awarded damages in millions as punitive damage and compensatory damages.[72]

From the above premise, it can be concluded that however there was a dissenting opinion in the above mentioned case by Justice Roberts. The theme that was portrayed by those signs and boards represented the overall characterisation of the society and did not relate to issues that were of private nature. It is seen that even hate speech on certain topics is protected under the First Amendment of the U.S. Constitution. Since the signs shown at the place constituted to be a public place, it was given the blanket immunity under the First Amendment clause. The compensation was awarded because the symbols portrayed hurtful messages and not because of those who were holding such boards and symbols. In United States, hate speech is also protected since it is deemed essential for a progressive American society and the debate in public sphere do not vanish as they are essential for a democratic setup.[73]

[1] George Brunn, *"Free speech and its limits"*, NEW YORK REVIEW OF BOOKS, Vol.39, (1992), p. 19.

[2] *Ibid.*

[3] T. Jarymowicz, "*Robert Post's theory of freedom of speech: A critique of the reductive conception of political liberty*", PHILOSOPHY & SOCIAL CRITICISM, Vol. 40(1), (2014), pp. 107–123.

[4] Jack M Balkin, "*Free Speech is a Triangle*", COLUMBIA LAW REVIEW, Vol. 118(7), (2018), at https://columbialawreview.org/content/free-speech-is-a-triangle, (Accessed on April 18, 2019).

[5] *Ibid.*

[6] 250 U.S. 616 (1919).

[7] T. Nettleton, "*The Philosophy of Justice Holmes on Freedom of Speech*", SOUTHWESTERN POLITICAL SCIENCE QUATERLY, Vol. 3(4), (1923), pp. 287-305, Available at http://www.jstor.org/stable/42883960, (Accessed on April 18, 2019).

[8] J.S. Mill, ON LIBERTY, The Floating Press, (2009), p. 87.

[9] *Ibid.*

[10] Alex Daniel, "*Speech Locked Up: John Locke, Liberalism and the Regulation of Speech*", SETON HALL LAW REVIEW, Vol. 43, (2013), p. 154.

[11] Jeremy Waldron, THE HARM IN HATE SPEECH, Harvard University Press (2012), p.4.

[12] *Ibid.*

[13] *Ibid.*

[14] *Id.*, at p. 65.

[15] Anne Weber, MANUAL ON HATE SPEECH, p. 1.

[16] Article 10 "*Freedom of expression*" (1) everyone has the right to freedom of expression. This right shall include freedom to hold opinions and to receive and impart information and ideas without interference by public authority and regardless of frontiers. This Article shall not prevent States from requiring the licensing of broadcasting, television or cinema

enterprises.

(2) The exercise of these freedoms, since it carries with it duties and responsibilities, may be subject to such formalities, conditions, restrictions or penalties as are prescribed by law and are necessary in a democratic society, in the interests of national security, territorial integrity or public safety, for the prevention of disorder or crime, for the protection of health or morals, for the protection of the reputation or rights of others, for preventing the disclosure of information received in confidence, or for maintaining the authority and impartiality of the judiciary.

[17] *Jersild v. Denmark* [GC], Series A No. 298, para 30.

[18] *Gündüz v. Turkey,* No. 35071/97, para 40, CEDH 2003-XI.

[19] Anne Weber, MANUAL ON HATE SPEECH, p. 2.

[20] *Ibid.*

[21] Article 11 "*Freedom of expression and information*" (1) Everyone has the right to freedom of expression. This right shall include freedom to hold opinions and to receive and impart information and ideas without interference by public authority and regardless of frontiers.

(2) The freedom and pluralism of the media shall be respected.

[22]*Ibid.*

[23] Anne Weber, MANUAL ON HATE SPEECH, p. 10.

[24] Michael Herz, THE CONTENT AND CONTEXT OF HATE SPEECH: RETHINKING REGULATIONS AND RESPONSES, Cambridge University Press (2012), p. 475.

[25] Russell Sandberg, RELIGION AND LEGAL PLURALISM, Routlegde (2016), p. 182.

[26]Article 19 INTERNATIONAL COVENANT OF CIVIL AND POLITICAL RIGHTS (ICCPR), 1966.

[27]*Ibid.*

[28] Article 20 (1) Any propaganda for war shall be prohibited by law.

(2) Any advocacy of national, racial or religious hatred that constitutes incitement to discrimination, hostility or violence shall be prohibited by law.

[29]*Ibid.*

[30] Article 19 (1) Everyone shall have the right to hold opinions without interference.

2. Everyone shall have the right to freedom of expression; this right shall include freedom to seek, receive and impart information and ideas of all kinds, regard less of frontiers, either orally, in writing or in print, in the

form of art, or through any other media of his choice.

3. The exercise of the rights provided for in paragraph 2 of this article carries with it special duties and responsibilities. It may therefore be subject to certain restrictions, but these shall only be such as are provided by law and are necessary: (a) For respect of the rights or reputations of others; (b) For the protection of national security or of public order (*ordre public*), or of public health or morals.

[31] *Ibid.*

[32] Anne Weber, MANUAL ON HATE SPEECH, p. 14.

[33] CCPR/550/1993 (1996).

[34] Article 7 All are equal before the law and are entitled without any discrimination to equal protection of the law. All are entitled to equal protection against any discrimination in violation of this Declaration and against any incitement to such discrimination.

[35] Article 29 (1) everyone has duties to the community in which alone the free and full development of his personality is possible.

(2) In the exercise of his rights and freedoms, everyone shall be subject only to such limitations as are determined by law solely for the purpose of securing due recognition and respect for the rights and freedoms of others and of meeting the just requirements of morality, public order and the general welfare in a democratic society.

(3) These rights and freedoms may in no case be exercised contrary to the purposes and principles of the United Nations.

[36] Russell Sandberg, RELIGION AND LEGAL PLURALISM, Routlegde (2016), p. 185.

[37]*Delfi AS v. Estonia*, Application no. 64569/09.

[38]*Handysidev. United Kingdom*, Application no. 5493/72(1976).

[39] Anne Weber, MANUAL ON HATE SPEECH, p. 22.

[40]*Ibid.*

[41]*Id.*, at p. 24.

[42] 9626 (2015) Derebus 45.

[43] Article 17 "*Prohibition of abuse of rights*": Nothing in this Convention may be interpreted as implying for any State, group or person any right to engage in any activity or perform any act aimed at the destruction of any of the rights and freedoms set forth herein or at their limitation to a greater extent than is provided for in the Convention.

[44] Anne Weber, MANUAL ON HATE SPEECH, pp. 23-24.

[45] *Ibid.*

[46] *Honsik v. Austria*, No. 25062/94, decision of the Commission of 18 October 1995.

[47] Anne Weber, MANUAL ON HATE SPEECH, p. 25.

[48] *Lehideux and Isorni v. France* [GC], judgment of 23 September 1998.

[49] *Glimmerveen and Hagenbeek v. the Netherlands*, Nos. 8348/78 and 8406/78, p. 187.

[50] *Jersild v. Denmark*, para. 35.

[51] *Anthony Norwood v. the United Kingdom*, Application no. 23131/03 (2004).

[52] Anne Weber, MANUAL ON HATE SPEECH, p.27.

[53] *Ibid.*

[54] *Vejdeland v. Sweden*, Application no. 1813/07 (2012).

[55] Section 16, CONSTITUTION OF SOUTH AFRICA.

[56] *Gloria Kentev.Andre van Deventer,* 9626 (2015) Derebus 45.

[57] *R. v.Keegstra,* (1990)3 SCR 697.

[58] *Ibid.*

[59] *R. v. Keegstra,* (1990)3 SCR 697.

[60] *Ibid.*

[61] 2013 1 SCR 467.

[62] Anne Weber, MANUAL ON HATE SPEECH, p.27.

[63] *Ross v. New Brunswick School District,* 1996 1 SCR 825.

[64] Abhinav Chandrachud, RHETORIC OF REPUBLIC: FREE SPEECH AND THE CONSTITUTION OF INDIA, Penguin Books (2017), p. 244.

[65] *Beauharnais v. People of the State of Illinois,* 343 US 250 (1952).

[66] *Village of Skokie v. Nationalist Socialist Party of America,* 562 US 443 (2011).

[67] Abhinav Chandrachud, RHETORIC OF REPUBLIC: FREE SPEECH AND THE CONSTITUTION OF INDIA, Penguin Books (2017), p. 246.

[68] *Ibid.*

[69] No. 740309.

[70] 505 US 377 (1992).

[71] *Ibid.*

[72] *Snyder v. Phelps,* 562 US 443 (2011).

[73]Abhinav Chandrachud, RHETORIC OF REPUBLIC: FREE SPEECH AND THE CONSTITUTION OF INDIA, Penguin Books (2017), pp. 246-247.

CHAPTER THREE

REGULATORY MECHANISM OF FREEDOM OF SPEECH AND EXPRESSION

3.1 Introduction

This chapter deals with various Constitutional and penal provisions that are in place for tackling the menace of hate speech. The Constitutional perspective gives us insight about the manner in which the framers drafted the instrument keeping in mind the gloomy past and the requirements of that time with the hope that these provisions act as a guiding principle in the future when the need for reforms is felt. Election laws are also mentioned along with case laws that deal with this matter. The Procedural aspect of handling these provisions is mentioned as per the provisions laid down in the Code of Criminal Procedure. Similarly, substantive laws have also been mentioned citing judicial pronouncements. Minority rights protection related act and its provisions that help in eliminating hate speech are mentioned with reference to untouchability as an offence.

3.2 Freedom of Speech and Expression under Indian Constitution

The Right to Freedom of Speech and Expression is laid down under Article 19(1)(a) and is available to Indian citizens only. Citizens can exercise their right to propagate their ideas and in furtherance of dissemination of their ideas, publish and circulate it. Our Constitution does not entail restrictions in an arbitrary manner but provides such restrictions specifically under sub clause (2) of Article 19. There are eight restrictions upon the exercise of this right. There are penal laws in India that criminalise hate speech which have been specifically dealt with in further chapters. In plethora of cases these provisions have been challenged on the basis of their Constitutionality but the Supreme Court has held them to be consistent with Constitution.[1]

"Article 19(1)(a) reads as follows: Protection of certain rights regarding freedom of speech, etc.-

1. *All citizens shall have the right:*

a. *To freedom of speech and expression. Any limitation on this right must be a 'reasonable restriction' falling within the contours of Article 19(2)".*[2]

The restrictions are contained under Article 19(2) and it reads as follows:

"Nothing in sub-clause (a) of clause (1) shall affect the operation of any existing law, or prevent the State from making any law, in so far as such law imposes reasonable restrictions on the exercise of the right conferred by the said sub-clause in the interests of the sovereignty and integrity of India, the security of the State, friendly relations with foreign States, public order, decency or morality, or in relation to contempt of court, defamation, or incitement to an offence".[3]

Reasonability is the most important factor while putting restriction upon free speech, as the restrictions imposed upon must be reasonable and not at the whims and caprice of the State. Public order is the reason for providing blanket to most of the existing hate speech laws. There are other grounds such has morality, decency and incitement to an offence that save hate speech laws.[4] The Apex Court has held that limitations to basic freedoms can be viewed as reasonable only in extreme circumstances and judicial conformity cannot be used as a general rule.[5]

3.2.1 Hate Speech vis-a-vis Reasonable Restrictions

It is an established fact that the restrictions provided under Article 19(2) are exhaustive and therefore, no other ground can be used for curtailing the right to freedom of speech and expression. Most importantly, the restrictions imposed should be reasonable and not imposed arbitrarily. The phrase, "in the interests of" which is present before the grounds for restriction makes way for anticipatory action which is often cited as a preventive measure.

In order to be accepted by various realms of a democratic setup, such as the judiciary and the will of the people, any law should be substantively and procedurally reasonable. If it appears to be arbitrary or if it is excessively exercised, then such law cannot have the support it requires being in force anymore. Thus, it can be challenged on the ground of unreasonableness. While putting these restrictions due care has to be taken with regard to the nature of the restrictions being imposed and the evil sought to be curbed. Furthermore, disproportion caused and the conditions prevalent during the period in which such restriction is being imposed needs to be taken note of.[6] Every statute that has been challenged should be tested for reasonability as no straight jacket formula can be applied to such cases.[7]

3.2.2 *'In the interests of'*

This particular phrase paves way for prior restraint or anticipatory action on speech, though it still has to confirm to the requirements of Article 19[8], it has been read to establish a close relationship between actual restrictions imposed under exception of Article 19(2). In *Ramji Lal Modi*[9] case, the apex court has laid down that a law could be read into 'in the interests of' public order even though it may not deal with 'public order'.

The stance in *Ramji Lal Modi* changed in the case of *Superintendent, Central Prison, Fatehgarh v. Dr Ram Manohar Lohia*[10] (*Lohia-I*). The court held that there should be rationale nexus between the restrictions imposed and the evil sought to be weeded out.[11]

3.2.3 *'Public Order' under Article 19(2)*

The first amendment brought into the ambit of reasonable restrictions the term 'public order'. Before this introduction in 1951, section 153A of Indian Penal Code that dealt with the issue of class hatred was declared unconstitutional due to the fact that it was not a restriction. Thus public order saved an important hate speech. This term also held section 295 of IPC to be valid when was challenged in Ramji Lal Modi as the court held that the restriction helped in curtailing criminal activities that tend to create public disorder. As per the judicial interpretation just mentioned, it deems fit that any provisions that deal with hate speech laws should be judged as per the evolution of the society and the standards that have been set as judicial precedents.[12]

In this context, public order restriction has been held to be such that it tends to protect any activity that may cause public disorder. It however does not matter whether such disorder has been caused or not as this happens to be of precautionary nature. Furthermore, if the speech tends to cause grave discontent amongst the masses with regard to their feelings towards their religion, such speeches needed to be curbed at the earliest.

In *Virendra*[13], the Court took the stance that no presumptions are to be arrived at when the State imposes reasonable restrictions and only the action carried out by the state has to be looked into and not the statue from where such actions derive their power. It further extended this view of Lohia I wherein it held that 'public order' would also include public peace and tranquillity with relation to local needs and importance. State is the foremost authority for the safety and well being of the citizens and hence only actions that have observed procedural guidelines and rules are to be challenged and not those that question the statute itself.

The restrictions imposed in the interests of public order are reasonable only when it has an object sought to be achieved with particular relation to public order and not something which is nowhere to be related to the object. Hence, a rationale nexus is of utmost importance when restrictions are imposed upon the freedom of speech and expression. Following Lohia-I, two important judgments of the Supreme Court shed light upon what constitutes violation of 'public order'. One of the very first few cases is *Ram Manohar Lohia v. State of Bihar*[14](Lohia II), wherein the Apex Court cleared the air with regard to expressions used as reasonable restrictions such as 'public order' 'security of state'. The case was indirectly related to Article 19(2) as the court was contemplating upon the term 'public order' to which the court presented it reasoning as follows:

"One has to imagine three concentric circles. Law and order represents the largest circle within which is the next circle representing public order and the smallest circle represents security of State. It is then easy to see that an act may affect law and order but not public order just as an act may affect public order but not security of the State".[15]

3.2.4 Other significant judgments

The Supreme Court is the ultimate check on absolute power as it is the highest court in our judicial and democratic setup. The Apex Court has been widely criticised for the manner in which it has interpreted the restrictions imposed upon the exercise of individual's right to speech and expression. In Virendra, the court observed that it was impossible to create a universal standard in this context. There has been considerable development in the tests evolved for determining the legitimacy of restrictions on the pretext of 'public order'. Although, the judiciary has read together all the cases where 'public order' is involved in this context and has interpreted depending upon the circumstances of each and every individual case. Recently, *Subramanian Swamy v. Union of India* [16](*Subramanian Swamy*) has been widely criticised because it has interpreted restrictions in a broad manner while the Apex court has been lauded for its judgment in *Shreya Singhal*[17], which has set in stone the role of judiciary as protector of fundamental freedom to speech and expression.

On the issue of 'public order' the Constitutional Bench of the Apex Court has decided the above mentioned various case laws which largely focus upon the reasonableness. Now, we shall discuss cases that demonstrate its application.

Supreme Court in 1989 case of *Rangarajan*[18]emphasised that speech should be restricted only if it hampers public interest in a dangerous manner. The proximity test laid down in Lohia-I was followed in this case to lay down that the expression and the action resulting thereon should be read together like the equivalent of a spark in a powder barrel.

While in 2016 judgment of *Shreya Singhal v. Union of India*[19](*Shreya Singhal*) that dealt with online hate speech, Supreme Court had developed its own jurisprudence to cater the needs of modern technological times. The court held that while deciding cases related to violation of 'public order' a question needs to be asked that whether the act concerned would cause any disturbance in the community or it only effects the individual, leaving the community intact and undisturbed. It relied upon the difference between discussion, advocating thoughts and incitement to violence. Discussion and propagation of one's thoughts is the central idea of freedom of speech and expression as given under Article 19(1) (a) and the clause (2) would come in play only when speech leads to incitement to an offence. It relied upon the tendency test, proximity test, as well the reasoning of the 1989 position.[20]

In *Pravasi Bhalai Sangathan*[21] case the Apex Court delved deep into to look out for the need for provisions to curtail hate speech. The court held that it is not only necessary but the need of the hour that such restrictions are placed upon hate speech that tend to create differences and discrimination in the society. The aim is to provide protection to the minorities and those that have been subject to social exclusion and have been marginalised by such adverse behaviour. Such behaviour is resultant due to the environment created by inflammatory speeches made in public domain that leads to dissemination of hatred amongst the communities.

3.3 Elections Laws and Hate Speech

Free and fair election is a basic and essential feature in a democracy. The provision for conduct of elections is provided in the Articles 324 to 329 of the Indian Constitution along with the Representation of People's Act, 1951 (from here on referred as RoPA); and other rules contained in Conduct of Election Rules, 1961. The right to freedom of speech and expression is greatly in conflict with the reasonable restrictions during the election season as vigorous exercise of this right may tantamount to its violations and hence the right ends up being curtailed. RoPA contains provisions that disqualify the candidature of the candidate and criminalise speeches that fall under the category of corrupt practices and electoral offences respectively. Clause 3A of Section 123 of the RoPA deals with the former while Section 125 deals with the latter issue.

3.3.1 Electoral Corrupt Practices vis-a-vis Hate Speech

Section 123(3A)[22] was brought forth in 1961 amendment to the RoPA in order to complement Section 153A of IPC with a specific purpose of putting a check upon violation of freedom of speech during the elections. In order to prevent any speech that creates communal divide or divide on the basis of regionalism or cast, this section was brought as has been held in the case of *Ramesh Yeshwant Prabhoo*[23].Such speech is specifically dealt with under clause 3A of the said section and it was the need of the hour to have a provision that protects the secular and democratic character of the country.

Justifying the need for this provision, the apex court in *Ziyauddin Bukhari*[24] has said the following:

"It is evident that, if such propaganda was permitted here, it would injure the interests of members of religious minority groups more than those of others. It is forbidden in this country in order to preserve the spirit of equality, fraternity, and amity between rivals even during elections. Indeed, such prohibitions are necessary in the interests of elementary public peace and order".

Ingredients of Section 123(3A)

i. **Act by a candidate or through his agent**

Consent of the candidate being paramount for speech to amount as a corrupt practice, sub section 3A of the Section 123 criminalises such speech if it is made by the candidate himself or by his agent on prior consent of the candidate. If such speech is made before the candidate has filed his candidature, it would not amount to an offence under the said section. Implied consent can be construed to if the candidate is present while such speech is being delivered.[25]

i. **Likely effect of speech**

For ensuring a landslide victory in the election, candidate often exercise their right to speech in a manner that is first targets the opposite political party but later such candidate resorts to deplorable speech that ends up promoting hatred among classes of citizens on the lines of religion, caste or descent. Hence, the perspective of the audience or the likely effect of speech on the voters is something that is a determining factor while holding a speech as hate speech.[26]

In above mentioned case, the speaker pleaded in election campaign on the basis of his religion, stating that his adversary was not a true follower of Islam. Supreme Court held that the language used by the speaker when measured against the given circumstance was evident enough to bring to its notice that such pleading or appeal was reckless and uncontrolled and was given to motivate hostile feelings between diverse classes present in the country.[27]

The Apex court while deciding the case of *Ebrahim Suleiman Sait*[28] held that if the likely effect of the speech is such that it promotes enmity between various classes present in this diverse nation, then it would attract the provisions of sub section 3A. It was alleged by the appellants that provocative speech was given against a political party and not towards any class of citizens as is the case under the provision. Although in the present case, the court did not find such proposition to be true as against the provisions of the said section.

"It seems to us that the speech sought to criticise the wrong policy of the Muslim League (Opposition) in aligning with parties that were allegedly responsible for atrocities against the Muslims and not just to emphasise the atrocities. In our opinion it cannot be said that the speech falls within the mischief of Section123(3A) of the Act; we have reached this conclusion keeping in mind the well established principle that the allegation of corrupt practice must be proved beyond reasonable doubt".

The Apex court held in *Ramesh Yeshwant Prabhoo*[29] that just by referring to a religion during a speech would not attract the provisions under section 123. The words in conflict should be read in the background or the circumstances surrounding the complete speech and not in a theoretical or text book manner.

Considering this matter in the recent judgment of *Pravasi Bhalai Sangathan v. Union of India*[30], the Supreme Court has held that the words used during speech and effects resulting thereon must be judged as per the standards of an ordinary prudent man, having a reasonable understanding, strong mind and courage to take in views not as per expectation. These are not to be judged keeping in mind the weak and feeble minded men who cannot take even the slightest form of dissenting opinions.

In *Ziyauddin Bukhari*[31], the Apex Court took its stand in favour of the 'likely effects test'. In relation to this, the Court held that one has to determine the outcome of speeches made by the candidate or by his agent in election period keeping in mind the average voter's mind and feelings in each and every case concerned with allegations of electoral corrupt practices.

3.3.2 Class hatred

Sub-section 3A deals with the provision to tackle the problem of promotion of feeling of hatred or enmity amongst various classes of citizens. In a particular case, *Rao Deshmukh*[32] where the appeal was filed contending that if during election campaigning any appeal is made for 'Hindutwva' it does not mean that appeal is directed only towards one particular community. Furthermore, the appeal was made with regard to the followers of Hindu religion and the treatment they have subject to so far and was not aimed at creating any difference amongst the citizens. But the judiciary did not divulge further into this specific issue and came to a conclusion based on merits.

The judicial interpretation of such speeches is that usage of 'Hindutwva' or 'Hindus' does not refer to people on the basis of religion. The Court even went to the extent of saying that there cannot be a fixed meaning to this word and it cannot be just restricted to periphery of religion. It is a way of life, which has been linked to 'Indianisation' and the speech has to be judged in its entirety and not just limiting the scope to use of this word in order to see whether such speech is segregating people on the pretext of religion.[33]

The use of Hindutwva during speeches was again considered in *Manohar Joshi*[34] case where candidate relied on usage of this word as a basis for establishment of a Hindu state. The Apex Court held that this cannot be said to be violative of Section 123(3A) as this is not dividing people but is just a glimpse of hope.

But in 2017, a final decision on this particular issue was reached by in the case of *Abhiram Singh*[35] wherein it was held that no appeal on the basis of religion would be permitted as elections are a secular function that was exercised in consonance with the various diversities prevailing in the country.

3.3.3 Yardstick for prosecuting Hate Speech violation cases

Just like criminal procedure, any such alleged violation of hate speech laws during elections needs to be proved beyond reasonable doubt and they cannot be proved by prevailing possibilities. This has been observed as the penalty imposed under the various provisions is of severe nature. A candidate may lose his seat and can be further disqualified from contesting elections for six years.[36]

3.3.4 Truth as defence

The highest court of the land has settled the proposition in *Ebrahim Suleiman Sait*[37] that truth cannot be used as a defence in the case relating to speeches that promote hatred in the society. Even if the statements are based on facts, it would not save such statements from the provisions under the RoPA. The relevant test is that whether such statements promoted enmity amongst the society or not. If it does so create, then it is of no importance that the statements uttered were based on facts or not. It also becomes irrelevant when such statements were made out quite some time ago.

3.3.5 Constitutionality of Section 123(3A) vis-à-vis Articles 19(1)(A) and 25

Section 123(3A): The apex court for the first had taken in consideration the validity of Section 123(3A) in the case of *Ramesh Yeshwant Prabhoo*[38]. Finding it to be consistent with the Right to freedom of Speech and expression it held that this section falls within the ambit of reasonable restrictions, namely 'public order' and also 'incitement to an offence'. The detriment effect on public order is caused due to the various clauses present under the said section. Promoting enmity or hatred is clearly barred as per the said section and any such activity has a detrimental effect on the society and creates further divide among the communities.

3.3.6 Section 125 of RoPA: Electoral Offences

Section 125[39] of the act deals with the provision that deals with the issue of promotion of enmity between the classes during the election process. It provides a punishment that includes imprisonment up to three years, or fine or both if any person involved in the election promotes or even attempts to promote enmity on the grounds of religion, race, caste, community or on linguistic basis.[40]

3.3.7 Electoral Hate Speech versus Penal Hate Speech

Consequences: There is a difference of element between the provisions dealing with Hate Speech contained under section 123 and 125. It may on the face appear to be same, but are different in the consequences resulting on its enforcement. The latter creates criminal consequences for the person violating further making it more viable than the former since cognizance for it can be taken under Criminal Procedure while for the former it can be taken place only after announcement of the election results.[41]

Ingredients of offences: The ingredients of both sections are different as under Section 123(3A) the act must have been performed by the agent or the candidate himself for benefitting the candidate or to the detriment of his opponent. While section 125 forsakes the motive behind the commission of the offence and takes into the person guilty of committing such act.

The Supreme Court, in *Ebrahim*[42] case as well as in another case has brought forth the element that makes both the sections different from each other in certain aspects.

"To attract 123(3A) the act must be done by the candidate or his agent or any other person with the consent of the candidate or his agent and for the furtherance of the election of that candidate or for prejudicially affecting the election of any candidate, but under section 125any person is punishable who is guilty of such an act and the motive behind the act is not stated to be an ingredient of the offence".[43]

Critics have suggested that the conduct of the candidate prior to the nomination should also be taken into consideration while judging on the pedestal of both these provisions. It has been laid down by apex court[44] that candidate attains official status only on the day he files his nomination papers. Therefore, he can be only penalised under these sections only if he is a candidate. It has been on many occasions observed that candidates give speeches that have been coloured with religious spirits which tend to create an atmosphere of divide amongst the voters much before they file their candidature, hence are saved from the clutches of these provisions. It is therefore in the best interests for a modern Indian democracy that activities of candidates a year prior to their nomination should be taken in cue for adjudging their conduct.[45]

3.4 Code of Criminal Procedure

3.4.1 Section 95 and Section 96

There are provisions that enable the State to take preventive action and take guard against any form of act that undermines the overall well being of a society. In this connection, literature or books and newspapers are one of the mediums of communication that are often subject to prior restraint being acted against their circulation by the authorities. This is done so as to curb any element of hate speech related content that may cause distress in the society if it reaches the readers.

In this regard, there are two provisions of Cr.PC, section 95 and 96 respectively that give permission to the State authority to forfeit any form of document or book or even newspaper if such publication purports to offences related to sedition, promoting enmity between classes and promotion of enmity between people on the basis of religion. These provisions grant power specifically to the State government to forfeit such literature that carries with itself any type of hate speech.[46]

This action of confiscation of the material related to hate speech is carried out by the Police personnel. If the order for confiscation has to remain good in law, then it has to observe certain postulates. These so mentioned postulates were mentioned by the Supreme Court in the case that dealt with the forfeiture of the book '*Ramayana: A True Reading*'. This was the case of *Lalai Singh Yadav*.[47]

The first one is that the material so confiscated should depict that it had matter that could create tensions between different classes in the society. In the case of *Arun Ghose*[48], the order for confiscation was held to be bad in law as it did not classify the classes that would have been at helm of enmity between them.

In another case that dealt with the book of '*Shivaji*', the Apex court held the order to be correct as it had been established that there existed two classes that could have been at each other's throat if the book had not been forfeited. The classes were: the one that were the staunch supporters of king Shivaji and the other one that did not follow him as their supporter.[49]

Secondly, the order so given to the police should mention as to the grounds on which the government has ordered the material to be confiscated. The above judgment has been re-iterated in other cases which mention that the notification so issued has to carry the government's clear and precise order.[50]

Thirdly, the grounds on which the order has been issued should be clear and precise and there should not be an iota of doubt. It is laid down that merely mentioning the ingredients of section 95 in the order is understood not to be sufficient and demands grounds in detail.[51]

Lastly, there exists a potential difference between grounds on which government has soughted the material to be taken and the grounds for action that the police shall take. In the famous case that involved the elements of section 95 is the case that involving the script titled: '*I am Nathuram Godse Speaking*'. It was supposed to be a part of the play of the same name. The High Court of Bombay held that the grounds mentioned did not qualify to attract the provisions of the said section. This was due to the fact that the play was cited to create enmity between different groups such that it would create public disorder. But the court held that the ground was insufficient such that it only mentioned the ingredients of IPC and mere re-phrasing the section would not be sufficient to constitute the forfeiture as character of the act has to be mentioned.[52]

3.4.1.1 Factors taken into consideration to invoke provision

Historical works offer varying deliberation and usually do not attract the criteria mentioned under section 95. Any work has to be seen as a whole in order to constitute the order of forfeiture. The courts as seen in many cases refers to the work and scrutinises the content and sees the content of the work as a whole and does not refer to any specific part of the same.

3.4.1.2 Content of the published work

If the content of the published work in issue has some data that has likelihood that it could constitute the work as a provocative work then the difference between in the content and the manner in which it has been written makes way for constituting whether it attracts the provision or not. In case if the work seems to contain text that seems to pose problem but if overall the work is containing meek and clement language then such order for forfeiture can be set aside by the courts. This was done in the case of *Shivram Das*[53] where the above mentioned proposition was iterated by the court.

3.4.1.3 Works containing Historical content

Historical works that may be true but if they have the potential to create divide amongst the citizens, then defence of past true events cannot be implied under section 153A of IPC. The stance of the judiciary has been that if the works that deal with historical instances have the content that may cause problem or it might not and these sorts of works can be taken as an exception. The above held proposition was held in the case of *Varsha Publications*[54] wherein it was stated that it was Hindu religion that had made its effect in the Middle east prior to the Islamic era. It was contended that work by the author was researched and based on references of researchers. The court held that this was case that involved the provision of IPC, namely section 153A and it has to be tested upon different tests laid down for that particular provision. Providing a complete ban can lead to violation of freedom of speech and expression as over banning has a negative effect.

Work in its entirety has to be taken into consideration and no pin point reference of the text can be taken as controversial. Unless the entire work promotes enmity, only then it can be forfeited else work seen in remoteness cannot be taken for invoking the said provision.

3.4.1.4 Can the forfeiture be challenged?

Under section 96A of CrPC, a remedy is available to the publisher whose work has been forfeited to challenge the said order. Any person other than publisher himself can also seek relief against the said order. Therefore, even a book owner also can claim relief as every Indian citizen has the right to information.[55]

If any person such as an advocate approaches the court with regard to appeal against the order of confiscation he has the locus standi for doing so. Social Activists are also within the ambit of locus standi. This was held in the case of *Sanghuruj*[56] which dealt with the book related to Shivaji was forfeited as it was alleged that such book could create enmity amongst citizens of the state. The question arose with regard to the locus standi of the appellants which comprised of a lawyer, a film maker and also a social activist.

The Apex Court has laid down precisely that the High Court's power of reviewing the order of forfeiture should be limited to the grounds that are mentioned when the order for same was passed. An example for the same could if the order for confiscation states that it involves the provisions of section 153A, the high court's review should be restricted to that specific section and it should not judge whether the text in question could draw other sections of the IPC. Similarly, if the order is completely silent on the grounds and it only narrate the ingredients of section 95 or IPC, the court must set aside such order as being invalid. In the case of *Virendra Bandhu*[57] the Rajasthan High Court laid down that the court cannot go beyond its power and look into the government's opinion by ordering an inquiry.

3.4.1.5 Constitutional Validity of Section 95and 96

It has been held by the judicial interpretation that the provisions regarding confiscation of the controversial material are sufficient in dealing with the problem of hate speech. The act of prior restricting the circulation of material lies within the ambit of government's power to maintain law and order in the society. Thus, if the provisions are followed after due diligence, there shall no violation of the fundamental right to free speech and expression. The right to challenge the forfeiture is also available as a remedy to publisher and other interested persons which makes it clear that the procedural safeguards are available to the aggrieved party. Thus, these sections are constitutionally valid.[58]

3.4.2 Section 144

Section 144 CrPC is one of the most infamous provisions that is prevalent since colonial times and has numerously times been used as a means to curb free speech. It has also been used for carrying out shutdown of Internet so as to prevent the spreading of false and inflammatory information. In order to be a valid order, the order executing the provisions of this section should satisfy certain postulates.[59]

Firstly and most importantly the command must be in writing and must not contain any ambiguity. This is done so far so to increase the sanctity of the order so issued and furthermore, the people who are denied the fundamental rights should know the exact things they have to abstain from. It must in absolute expression specify the 'persons, place and act' that are to be restrained.[60]

Secondly, the basis for the order so issues must be on the material facts and not on frivolous facts. In Ramlila Maidan incident, the request for organising the protest was granted and later the police on withdrawal of the above said grant lathi charged into the protest ground. The court said the orders were not correct as they were issued in an arbitrary manner. The apex court held that the execution of the orders under section 144 should be carried out on orders that specify the details without any ambiguity as the application of this section has direct consequences upon the individual's right to freedom of speech and expression.[61]

Thirdly, the order so issued must not extend beyond the period of two months and above all they should be issued in rarest of circumstances which display that there cannot be other alternate way to deal with such an acute situation. It should be issued in emergency situations only. The duration of the issued order must be co-extensive with the emergency that has to be dealt with. Thus it should be only issued if it provides for speedy remedy and at times of grave situations.[62]

3.4.2.1 Constitutional validity

It is often labelled as draconian law, colonial and tyrannical law. It has been extensively used as a means to curtail free speech and expression. The Constitutionality of section 144 has been brought forth in the case of *Babulal Parate*[63] which clearly laid down this provision to be in consonance with the Constitutional requirements. It was saved as under the provision of sub clause 2 of article 19 of the Indian Constitution which lay down instances in which reasonable restrictions can be imposed upon. Thus, in order to restore or preserve the public order, the section 144 comes in handy and thereby is held as Constitutional.

3.4.3 Preventive Detention Provisions under CrPC

The Criminal procedure code in India makes provisions for preventive detention under Section 107 and 151. The former is the provision that makes it possible for the authorities to arrest persons even before the event that poses threat to peace takes place. While the latter provision makes way for execution of the former provision. The nature of these provision is preventive and not of penalizing nature.[64]

The offences under IPC that deals with issue of hate speech such as section 153A and 295A, etc. are cognizable offences. Hence there arrest can be made by a police officer without any warrant. For execution of these substantive provisions, the procedure provides for section 151 that gives power to a police officer to make an arrest in cases where there is possibility of occurrence of any offence that is cognizable. Thus the instances where there is likelihood of occurrence of a hate speech offence, this section comes in play.[65]

Furthermore, both these sections make it available for the magistrate to impose bonds upon persons to maintain peace. The person arrested under section 151 can be arrested for a maximum period of 24 hours and not more than that. If there arose the need for keeping the person so arrested behind the bars beyond the prescribed time, then section 107 comes in play and has to be applied along with section 151. During the mass anti-corruption movement that was underway in the summer of 2011, section 151 was imposed to carry out the arrest of social reformer and activist Anna Hazare. This was done so as to prevent the protesting activist from breaking the law under section 144 of CrPC.[66]

In order to uphold the Constitutionality of the invoked provisions, it is necessary that certain postulates are followed while invoking these sections. Section 151 is divided into two parts that make it necessary for the authorities to comply with. First essential is the 'knowledge of design' and the second postulate is related to apprehension of occurrence of a cognizable offence that is 'imminent danger test'.[67]

In a case of Orissa where a person was so arrested as he had certain political links with a political party and was arrested as he was accused of allegedly have design to commit certain offences. However, the report of the police officer did not in way establish that the knowledge of design of the offence for which the accused was arrested and also failed to establish a nexus between the political party involvements with the said person. Likelihood of occurrence of an event is something different than full proof knowledge that such offence might be committed.[68]

If a political party has a history of getting involved in matters of public tranquillity, does not solely give the right to invoke this provision. The police officer was not able to establish a relation between the arrested person and the offence that was alleged to be committed.[69]

The second element that needs to be complied with is the 'imminent danger' test. Whenever there is an element of fear in the society, there are various rumours in the air. The authorities should not pay heed to such rumours rather should employ resources in sanctifying the available knowledge of apprehension of occurrence of an offence. Cognizable offences pose grave threat to person's life and liberty and hence the authorities should scrutinize the source of information before progressing for arrest of the persons. Hence, section 155 should be invoked when there is no recourse to other provisions. Similarly, section 107 should be invoked only when there is an emergency and no other possible way is left to tackle the apprehension of an offence.[70]

3.5 Indian Penal Code

3.5.1 Section 153B

This section specifically deals with the menace of statements that are aimed at thwarting the national unity of the country. An offence under section 153B is constituted when it satisfies the two main ingredients. Firstly, the section involves the issue of class and community. Secondly it involves the maker of the said statements.[71]

The maker of the statements not only includes the person making such statements but also any other person who repeats the inflammatory statements. 'Publication' simply implies the act of circulating or the act of making it known to other persons. Thus, the most important element of this section is the act of publishing the said statements. In order to attain the conviction for the offence under this section, it is vital that it is established that statements made were brought into the knowledge of a third party.[72]

People who have similar mindsets tend to socialise in the company similar to their beliefs. Often those who are similar minded are put in cross hairs so as to challenge their unity. The second vital ingredient of this section is the 'class of persons'. People who belong to a particular race or religion or have same linguistic traits constitute the term class of persons.[73]

The court in the *Murzban Shroff*[74] case of held as follows:

"Therefore, the said publication of the said assertion, appeal should relate to the said obligation. To give an illustration, in Sikh Religion, it is obligatory for Sikh to wear Turban and carry Kirpan or for Hindu not to eat cow meat or for Muslim to pray Namaz for five times in a day. It is apparent therefore that if the assertion, appeal pertains to any such obligation of the member of a religious group etc. and such a plea, appeal is likely to cause disharmony only then it would fall under sub-clause (c) of sub-section (1) of Section 153-B".

3.5.2 Section 295A

This provision penalises any act that are carried out to hurt the religious feelings of any person or class or community with a clear mindset to harm their religious feelings or their religious beliefs. It has been dealt in the history of hate speech in India in Chapter-I of this work. So apart from the historical background, the essential ingredients of this section are premeditated and malevolent intention.[75]

3.5.2.1 'Deliberate act'

The apex court in the case of Narain Das[76] explained the meaning of the term deliberate as follows:

"Where the intention to wound was not conceived suddenly in the course of discussion, but premeditated, deliberate intention may be inferred. Similarly, if the offending words were spoken without good faith by a person who entered into a discussion with the primary purpose of insulting the religious feelings of his listener's deliberate intention may be inferred".[77]

3.5.2.2 'Malicious intent'

Wrongful or malicious intent means an act whereby a person hurts another person without any justiciable cause. But if the statement so made that causes insult to any particular class of person is done so as so to bring about social reform in the society is excluded from the purview of malicious or wrongful intent. Furthermore, it should also be noted that in the name of criticism one cannot resort to usage of foul language.[78]

3.5.2.3 'Work to be read as whole'

Moreover, work should be seen as whole and not in particular portion that attracted the provision. Work should be given as liberal approach as possible keeping in mind the entire theme of the work and not a particular portion of the work. This was held by the apex court in the case of *Shailabala Devi*[79].

3.5.2.4 'Surrounding circumstances'

It is the foremost rational expectation from the judiciary that it should view the work keeping in mind the language used and facts and circumstances of the case. The theme or the central idea of the entire work constitutes the surrounding circumstances in which the work has been executed. In a famous case that dealt with the work of author Tasleema Nasrim, the court held that work should be judged on account of theme and in the present case, the intention of the author was to bring out the issues that long awaited plagued the society. Therefore, it was held to be not hit by this provision and subsequently, the order for confiscation of the book was also ruled out.[80]

3.5.2.5 'Words spoken or written'

In order to attract the provisions of this section, it is necessary that words must be either spoken or written or it should be in any form of visible representation. Caricature does not constitute the above said postulates laid down.[81]

3.5.2.6 'Outraging religious feelings'

It has held by the courts that the judiciary must perform the primary duty to judge cases by caution and not by getting involved in the issue of belief of any religion etc.[82]

3.5.2.7 Tests

Criterion for constituting outrage is an essential element of this provision as this provision involves bigger criterion. The outraging of the religious belief should be of the entire class and the feelings need to be harmed in a substantial manner. A certain section of people hurt would not enjoy protection under this section.[83]

Reasonable person test: It has to be adjudged from the audience involved. In order to constitute the offence, it has to be seen from the view point of strong minded and courageous men and not from the view point of weak and feeble minded men.[84]

3.5.2.8 Truth as defence

In our country due to various diversities and social norms, the option of exercising truth as a defence to one's own work cannot be used. In the *Rogdrigues*[85] case, the author had criticised the religious book of Christians, Holy Bible and mentioned that the Church for not adhering to the teachings that have been imparted in the holy book. The author went on to the extent of using abusive and foul language and was held liable for the same by the court as such work harmed the religious feelings of the followers of this religion.

3.5.2.9 Conclusion

The section has been upheld by the apex court as being constitutionally valid in the famous case of *Ramji Modi*[86] whichdealt with the issue of cow protection. The appellant was the editor of a magazine that carried a controversial article and was held to be hurting the devout followers of another community. However, he challenged the decision in the Supreme Court which upheld the provision as being within the permissible limits of clause 2 of article 19. The court cited a broader version of the restrictions imposed by employing the phrase 'in the interests of' rather than 'for the maintenance of'. As to the validity of this provision when pitted against freedom of religion, this provision holds good in law as the restriction can be imposed on the ground of 'public order'.

Comparison can also be drawn between Section 295A and 298. The former provision attracts stringent punishment and constitutes an offence of greater degree than the latter although they both appear to deal with the same issue. The main element that draws out distinction between both the provisions is that Section 295A has a wide ambit and deals with all mediums of expressions by which hate speech can be spread while Section 298 only attracts verbal speech. Furthermore, the former applies to classes of persons while the latter applies only to a person. Thus the former constitutes a graver offence than the latter. Both of these provisions are sufficient to tackle the menace of hate speech.[87]

3.6 Schedule Castes and Schedule Tribes (Prevention of Atrocities) Act, 1989

This specific act was enacted so as to uplift the members of the Schedule castes and schedule tribes (SC and ST) by granting them protection from certain acts of derogatory nature. This act paves way for holding any inflammatory or incendiary speech made against the members of these castes. There are four essential postulates that need to complied with in order to invoke the provision of Section 3(1)(x)[88] which criminalises any insult or intimidation carried out against them.[89]

Firstly, the persons accused of the offence should not belong to the SC/ ST community. Secondly, the accused was well aware that the complainant of the offence was a SC or ST. Thirdly, the accused has with deliberate intention or with a malicious intent used words to insult the members of these communities. Lastly, such an act of insult must have taken place in presence of public or 'public view'. Most importantly, it is the prosecution that has to prove the offence beyond reasonable doubt.[90]

The act must have been done with a deliberate and clear intention. This means that the act has to be purposefully carried out in order to insult a person because of status as member of this community.[91]

The use of caste slurs as a means to insult and cause harm to another person of that caste is an offence under this provision. The use of caste word 'Chamar' as a means to enrage or humiliate people belonging to that caste has been held to be as act that invokes this section. Use of this word is the same as in the United States the word 'nigger' is used.[92]

However if calling of caste name is not accompanied by the intention to bring out humiliation or insult to the addressed person, then such act does not attract the provisions of section 3(1)(x) of the SC/ST act. This is laid down in the case of *Subal Chandra Ghosh*[93] which is mentioned as below:

"It is a matter of common knowledge that such (abusive) words in a quarrel between the two enemies at a spur of moment are common and in routine and cannot possibly be taken to be an offence under the Act. That means, merely uttering such words in the absence of intention/ mens-rea to humiliate the complainant in public view, every such quarrel or altercation between the members of non-scheduled caste & scheduled caste and if the imputations are grossly vague and perfunctory, would not, ipso facto, constitute acts of commission of offence, which are capable of cognizance under the Act".

In order to constitute this offence, the insult has to be done in public view. What constitutes public is something that the judiciary has laid down in number of cases. One of them is *Asmathunnisa*[94] case, whereby the court held that even the entrance or the gate of the residence falls under the ambit of public view and even the garden that is visible from the surrounding road falls under this term.

There is another instance where the insult occurred on an online platform 'Facebook'. Here the cuss words relating to a cast were used, and the person who used such words had placed his profile as available to public. However, the person so accused presented his defence by stating that only his friends could view his posts and not everyone else or public for that matter. The court laid down that public includes people however small in number they may be and distribution of casteist comments and views on social and online platforms such as Facebook or WhatsApp would constitute public view. However, in the present case, the offence was not held to have taken place since the views expressed were regarding the community at large and not to specific persons thereby not qualifying as per the essential ingredients of the section.[95]

Thus, it can be concluded that hate speech with regard to minorities has been deal sufficiently by the present legal framework and is a distinct feature as compared to other provisions. Apart from the IT Act, various media laws in place in the country have been mentioned. However, it largely depends on the efficient administration since the onus of establishing and proving offence beyond reasonable doubt lies in the hands of government.

3.7 Hate speech and Civil Rights Act

Article 17 that abolishes untouchability has an enacted legislation to prevent any such acts under the Protection of Civil Rights Act, 1955. Section 7 of this act prescribes punishment for any attempt or an act of insulting a person who belongs to scheduled cast on the pretext of Untouchability. Furthermore, provoking or inciting people to start the practice of untouchability towards a class of person or towards a community also constitutes an offence under this section.

Although a mere to reference by caste name would not attract the provisions of this section. If one calls by the reference to caste such 'Mahar' or 'Harijan' this would not constitute the offence since there is no intent was not to insult on the pretext of untouchability. Section 7(1)(c) deals with the issue of encouragement of practice of untouchability, while section 7(1)(d) deals with the issue with respect to insult against schedule caste.[96]

Mens rea has not been used anywhere in the section but the Bombay High Court in the case of *Laxman Jayaram*[97] has made it clear that there must presence of mens rea in order to establish the offence under the provisions of section 7 of the said act.

From the above propositions, it can be concluded that this provision does not completely tackle the menace of hatred and discrimination in the society. Since, the judicial interpretation has brought mens rea into the reading of the bare provision; it is difficult to establish the offence. Thus, there needs to be reform in this provision as the burden of proof is on the prosecution and the complainant has less say in this.

3.8 Hate Speech and Dignity of Women

Women have been subject to derogatory remarks due to the prevalent description about them and their sexuality through the medium of advertisements, literature, etc. To tackle this problem, there is an enacted legislation present in the form of 'Indecent Representation of Women (Prohibition) Act, 1986'.

If there are instances where women are depicted in a derogatory manner and such manner could deprave or corrupt the minds of male in the society then this would attract the provisions of this act. The suo moto action taken by Rajasthan High court lays down that the television channels can curtail such indecent representation of women by regulating the content on their channels.[98]

Thus, it can be understood from the above mentioned para that women in a society have been stereotyped in a specific manner and that when people are subject to such stereotypical advertisements or television shows, they might act in manner that could lead to commission of crimes.

[1] *Sakal Papers (P) Ltd v. Union of India,* 1962 SCR (3) 842.

[2] Article 19, CONSTITUTION OF INDIA, 1950.

[3] *Ibid.*

[4] Gautam Bhatia, OFFEND, SHOCK OR DISTURB: FREE SPEECH UNDER THE INDIAN CONSTITUTION, Oxford University Press (2016), p. 159.

[5] *State of Madras v. V.G. Row,* 1952 SCR 597.

[6] *Chintaman Rao v. The State of Madhya Pradesh,* 1950 SCR 759.

[7] *Virendra v. State of Punjab,* AIR 1957 SC 836.

[8] *Babulal Parate v. State of Maharashtra,* 1961 SCR (3) 423.

[9] *Ramji Lal Modi v. State of UP,* AIR 1957 SC 620.

[10] *Superintendent, Central Prison, Fatehgarh v. Dr. Ram Manohar Lohia,* (1960) 2 SCR 82.

[11] *Ibid.*

[12] *Ramji Lal Modi v. State of UP,* AIR 1957 SC 620.

[13] *Virendra v. State of Punjab,* AIR 1957 SC 836.

[14] *Ram Manohar Lohia v. State of Bihar*, AIR 1966 SC 740, para 65.

[15] *Ibid.*

[16] W.P. (Crl) 184 of 2014.

[17] *Shreya Singhal v. Union of India*, (2015) 5 SCC 1.

[18] *S. Rangarajan v. P. Jagjivan Ram*, 1989 SCC (2) 574.

[19] 2015 5 SCC 1.

[20] *Ibid.*

[21] *Pravasi Bhalai Sangathan v. Union of India*, (2014) 11 SCC.

[22] Section 123(3A), REPRESENTATION OF PEOPLE'S ACT, 1951.

[23] *Dr. Ramesh Yeshwant Prabhoo v. Prabhakar Kashinath Kunte*, (1996) 1 SCC 130.

[24] *Ziyauddin Bukhari v. Brijmohan Mehra*, (1976) 2 SCC 17.

[25] *Ramakant Mayekar v. Smt Celine D'Silva*, 1996 SCC (1) 399.

[26] *Ziyauddin Bukhari v.Brijmohan Mehra*, (1976) 2 SCC 17.

[27]V.S. Rama Devi and S.K. Mendiratta, HOW INDIA VOTES: ELECTION LAWS, PRACTICE AND PROCEDURE, Lexis Nexis, (2014), p. 957.

[28] *Ebrahim Suleiman Sait v. M.C. Muhammad*, 1980 SCR (1)1148, para 2.

[29] *Dr. Ramesh Yeshwant Prabhoo v. Prabhakar Kashinath Kunte*, (1996) 1 SCC 130.

[30] 11 SCC 477, para 10.

[31] *Ziyauddin Bukhari v. Brijmohan Mehra*, (1976) 2 SCC 17.

[32] *Das Rao Deshmukh v. Kamal Kishore Nanasahebkadam*, 1995 SCC (5) 123.

[33]V.S. Rama Devi and S.K. Mendiratta, HOW INDIA VOTES: ELECTION LAWS, PRACTICE AND PROCEDURE, Lexis Nexis, (2014), pp. 976-978.

[34] *Manohar Joshi v.Nitin Bhaurao Patil*, (1996) 1 SCC 169.

[35] *Abhiram Singh v. C.D. Comachen*, C.A. No. 37/1992.

[36] *Borgoram Deuri v. Premodhar Bora*, C.A. No. 1300/2003.

[37] *Ebrahim Suleiman Sait v. M.C. Muhammad*, 1980 SCR (1)1148, para 4.

[38] *Dr. Ramesh Yeshwant Prabhoo v. Prabhakar Kashinath Kunte*, (1996) 1 SCC 130.

[39] Section 125 "*Promoting enmity between classes in connection with election*"—Any person who in connection with an election under this Act promotes or attempts to promote on grounds of religion, race, caste,

community or language, feelings of enmity or hatred, between different classes of the citizens of India shall be punishable, with imprisonment for a term which may extend to three years, or with fine, or with both.

[40] *Ibid.*

[41] *Ebrahim Suleiman Sait v. M.C. Muhammad,* 1980 SCR (1)1148, para 6.

[42] *Ibid.*

[43] *Ziyauddin Bukhari v. Brijmohan Mehra,* (1976) 2 SCC 17.

[44] *Indira Nehru Gandhi v. Raj Narain,* AIR 1975 SC 2299.

[45] *Harjit Singh Mann v.Umrao Singh,* AIR 1980 SC 701.

[46] Section 95,CODE OF CRIMINAL PROCEDURE, 1973.

[47] *State of Uttar Pradesh v. Lalai Singh Yadav.*

[48] *Arun Ranjan Ghose v. State of West Bengal,* (1955) Cr LJ 1002.

[49] *Sangharaj Damodar v. Nitin Gadre,* (2007) Cr LJ 3860.

[50] *Ibid.*

[51] *Ibid.*

[52] *Anand Chintamani Dighe v. State of Maharashtra,* (2002) 1 (Bombay CR) 57.

[53] *Shivram Dass Udasin v. State of Punjab,* AIR 1955 AIR P H 28.

[54] *Varsha Publications v. State of Maharashtra,* (1983) Cr LJ 1446.

[55] Section 96. CODE OF CRIMINAL PROCEDURE, 1973.

[56] *Sangharaj Damodar v. Nitin Gadre,* (2007) Cri LJ 3860.

[57] *Virendra Bandhu v. State of Rajasthan,* AIR 1980 Raj 24, para 5.

[58] *State of Uttar Pradesh v. Lalai Singh Yadav,* (1977) 1 SCR 616, para 9.

[59] Section 144, CODE OF CRIMINAL PROCEDURE, 1973.

[60] B.B. Mitra, CODE OF CRIMINAL PROCEDURE, Kamal Law House, (2011), p. 601.

[61] *Ibid.*

[62] B.B. Mitra, CODE OF CRIMINAL PROCEDURE, Kamal Law House, (2011), p. 603.

[63] *Babulal Parate v. State of Maharashtra,* (1961) 3 SCR 423.

[64] Section 107, CODE OF CRIMINAL PROCEDURE, 1973.

[65] Section 151, *ibid.*

[66] *RamlilaMaidan Incident v. Home Secretary, Union of India,* (2012) 5 SCC 1.

[67] B.B. Mitra, CODE OF CRIMINAL PROCEDURE, Kamal Law House, (2011), p. 537.

[68] *Prahlad Panda v. Province of Orissa,* AIR 1950 Ori 107.

[69] *Ibid.*

[70] B.B. Mitra, CODE OF CRIMINAL PROCEDURE, Kamal Law House, (2011), p. 538.

[71] Section 153B, INDIAN PENAL CODE, 1860.

[72] *Ibid.*

[73] Batuk Lal, COMMENTARY ON THE INDIAN PENAL CODE, Orient Publishing Co., (2013), p. 663.

[74] *Murzban Shroff v. State of Maharashtra,* Criminal Application No.992 of 2010 (Bombay).

[75] Section 295A, INDIAN PENAL CODE, 1860.

[76] *Narayan Das v. State of Orissa,* AIR 1952 Orissa149, para 7.

[77] *Ibid.*

[78] Batuk Lal, COMMENTARY ON THE INDIAN PENAL CODE, Orient Publishing Co., (2013), p. 1009.

[79] *State of Bihar v. Shailabala Devi,* AIR 1952 SC 329.

[80] Batuk Lal, COMMENTARY ON THE INDIAN PENAL CODE, Orient Publishing Co., (2013), pp. 1008-1011.

[81] *Ibid.*

[82] *Ibid.*

[83] T. Bhattacharya, INDIAN PENAL CODE, Central Law Agency, (2004), pp. 334-335.

[84] *Ibid.*

[85] *The State of Mysore v. Henry Rodrigues,* 1962 Cr LJ 564, para 5.

[86] *Ramji Lal Modi v. State of UP,* AIR 1957 SC 620, para 9.

[87] T. Bhattacharya, INDIAN PENAL CODE, Central Law Agency, (2004), pp. 334-335.

[88] Section 3(1)(x), SCHEDULE CASTES AND SCHEDULE TRIBES (PREVENTION OF ATTROCITIES) ACT, 1989.

[89] R.N. Chaudhary, COMMENTARY ON THE SCHEDULED CASTES AND SCHEDULED TRIBES ACT, Orient Publishing Company (2012), p. 64.

[90] *State of Karnataka v. Irrapa Hosamani* (2001) CrLJ 3566.

[91] *Swaran Singh v. State,* (2008) 8 SCC 435.

[92] *Ibid.*

[93] *Subal Chandra Ghosh v.State of West Bengal,* (2014) C.R.R. No. 2485.

[94] *Asmathunnisa v. State of Andhra Pradesh,* (2011) 11 SCC 259, para 9.

[95] *Gayatri v. State,* 2018 ALL MR(Cri)95.

[96] *SaritaDake v.Sr. Police Inspector*, 2008(3) MhL 385, para 14.

[97] *LaxmanJayaram v. State of Maharashtra*, 1981 Cri LJ 387.

[98] *Suo Moto v. State of Rajasthan* 2005AIR Raj 30.

CHAPTER FOUR

MEDIA REGULATIONS AND ONLINE HATE SPEECH

4.1 Introduction

This chapter deals with the provisions under the Information Technology Act, 2000 that criminalises the hate speech made on online platforms. Furthermore, various instances where the government has issued orders to shutdown the internet services has been dealt with reference to freedom of speech and expression. It is often seen that in cases where there is probability of communal divided or class hatred, the government orders closing of the internet services. Its aspects and its validity along with the responsibilities of intermediaries that are involved in providing internet services are herein mentioned in this chapter. The IT Act is the most prominent enactment that deals with the issue of online hate speech and the methods in which it can tackle these issues in spite of Section 66A of the Act being declared unconstitutional. Provisions that are dealt in this chapter include Section 69A and Section 79 of the Act. Medium of communication is of utmost importance when dealing with dissemination of multitudes of ideas and expressions. Thus, media laws have such as the Cable Television Regulations, the Cinematograph Act, the Programme Code and the role the department concerned with media, the Ministry of Information and Broadcasting plays are of vital importance when dealing with the issue of hate speech.

4.2Information Technology Act, 2000

Under this part, section 66A, Section 69A and Section 79 of the IT Act have been dealt with. These are mentioned as follows:

4.2.1 Section 66A Unconstitutional: Way Forward

This provision attracted media attention as this involved the arrest of two women where one of them had posted commenting on the efficacy of 'Bandhs' during the funeral march of a political leader while the other women had liked this post. This instance that took place during 2012 was finally settled by the apex court in the year 2015 in *Shreya Singhal*[2] case. The court in this case highlighted that the freedom of speech that is available to us in the 'offline' sphere holds the same position in the 'online sphere'.

On placing the impugned provision in the sight of fundamental freedom of speech and expression, the court declared that this section was violating the above right as it was not in proportion with the restrictions imposed. It went beyond the scope of restrictions that are present in Article 19(2). Moreover, lawless imminent action has been prescribed by the apex court as a means to employ charges against persons accused of any offences that relate to disruption of public order. If the judicial interpretation has to be looked into, it clearly mentions that mere causing annoyance cannot be a criterion for framing charges against citizens under this provision. After this decision, there was demand for the inclusion of provisions that were similar to Section 153A and 153B of the IPC.[3]

4.2.2 Section 69A

Information that is communicated through computers can be blocked or even taken down by the government if the circumstances create such a situation. The grounds on which such action can be soughted are if any content present online causes harm to 'public order'. Furthermore, if it deems necessary or it is of utmost importance then such an order can be issued. Therefore, if the provisions and the grounds laid down are not strictly adhered to, it can lead to the challenge of the order so issued.[4]

Another important aspect of this provision is to the authority that could issue and order for the taking down of content from the online platform or blocking any communication. With regard to this, there are blocking rules under the IT Act that prescribe certain rules that need to be complied with when issuing such orders. Moreover, any individual cannot just block the content but he has to approach the nodal officer for informing him about any such content that is spreading hatred or enmity in the society. The nodal offices of concerned ministries are the medium through which it shall go to the officer who has been assigned for such task.[5]

In emergency situations, the concerned officers approach the Department of Information Technology and on the approval of the department can issue the interim orders for blocking the content. Such issued interim orders are to be placed before a committee within the stipulated time period of 48 hours as per rule 9(3) of the blocking rules.[6]

The committee can also annul the temporary issued order and then order for the content so blocked to be unblocked. Any government department can request for the issue of such orders and usually it is the department of technology that has in many occasions issued such orders.[7]

Furthermore, there is also a Constitutional aspect attached to this section as it brings along with the option of judicial review which ensures impartiality and transparency. It is mentioned as per the rules that committee so constituted shall meet at least twice in a period of one month. This meeting shall ensure that the content so blocked has been done after following all the precautions and as per the laid down provision of the act. Such working groups constituted should exist foremost at the Union level of government and for efficient performance should be established at State levels too.[8]

4.2.2.1Constitutionality of Section 69A

It is of utmost importance that there is a hearing of the decision taken for blocking the content online prior to issue of such order. The person who has posted material online should be communicated by the authorities before such content has been taken down so as to give the opportunity to the maker of such content to present his case before the department that issues orders. The Constitutionality of the various rules under the IT Act was challenged in the previously mentioned case of *Shreya Singhal*[9]. Although the apex court has declined the contentions made in the case as there are ample safeguards present to not pervade the freedom of speech and expression.

However, the order issued must be done if it seems necessary to the government in order to maintain law and order. But the grounds for such should be within the ambit of reasonable restrictions that are specifically mentioned under Article 19(2) of the Constitution. Furthermore, the order issued must fulfil the procedural requirements such as the order must be written and the reason be mentioned so that it can go through the judicial scrutiny.[10]

With regard to the issue of pre decisional hearing, it is to be seen that the rules itself provide for the parties that are affected by the order to present their case before the committee that is constituted for reviewing its decision. Such safeguards are present so as to uphold the Constitutional aim envisaged by the framers of the Constitution.

4.2.3 Section 79

This section of the IT Act provides safe haven from criminal penalty to the service providers who offer their platform for online communications. Such protection is available if the posted content is done by third person and the immunity is granted upon fulfilment of certain conditions.[11]

There are certain pre-requisites that the intermediary needs to comply with. The foremost requisite being that he is only a medium for communication by offering online platform and not as a transmitter of information from his own end. Then he should not indulge into acts that could constitute 'transmission' and he should not 'modify', change or select the data that is transmitting on his platform. Lastly, he should observe caution while offering such platform as information has ripple effect that may go beyond control and cause disorder.[12]

It is to be noted that the service provider has to remove the content upon receiving notice from the court or if the government department issues any such orders. This would constitute that the provider now has the knowledge about the issue. Therefore, any other party that issues notice is beyond the scope of this act and hence does not compel the service provider to remove the content. Thus, if the intermediary has the information about the notice, he has to comply with such order and if he abstains from following such legal notice, he shall not be provided any immunity from criminal action against him.[13]

Thus, it can be concluded that online speech is regulated through various provisions of the IT Act and the rules contained therein. It is to be understood that India has tried to keep up with the prevailing rules and regulations that are enacted across the world. In this way, there is presence of government oversight on the online platform that can be used to spread hate speech messages and other inflammatory messages that could create gap or divide the communities. As mentioned above, the service providers have been tasked an important position to comply with the legal notice for blocking or removal of content from his platform in order to save himself from any criminal action. The first act from the government is precautionary and only after intermediaries does not comply then only criminal prosecution is initiated. Hence, it can be said that there is regulation of online hate speech although we lack in certain areas as pointed out by the parliamentary committees constituted to deal with the IT Act.[14]

4.3 Cable Television and Regulation Act, 1995

The period of 1990 was the time when the television started to pace up as a medium of entertainment in Indian households. In order to deal with the issues that started emanating with the advent of television and cable channels, it became necessary that such medium be regulated to maintain social harmony in the country. The Union government enacted this legislation and under this the Programme code. This code contains certain postulates that need to be complied by the channels airing content in the country. The most prominent regulations are Rule 6 of the code and Section 20 of the Act.

4.3.1 Rule 6

If there is any likelihood of particular content that could provoke or incite violence or could create law and order situation, this rule comes in play. If the channels are not in conformity of this rule, then such transmission is prohibited from being shown any further. Few instances related to violation of above rule and the government issuing notice for compliance with the code are: Sathiyam incident and the AajTak news channel incident.[15]

In the incident involving AajTak news channel, the channel had aired a conversation that pertained to some alleged terrorists following the repercussion of the death penalty of another terrorist. Rule 6 specifically prohibits any content that could create the problem of law and order and disrupt public order.[16]

In the Sathiyam incident, the southern based news channel had broadcasted a show that involved a interview with a religious preacher which had the likeliness of creating divide between the communities in the society. The ministry sent out a notice issuing warning for not complying with the provisions of the code.[17]

Regarding the issue of hate speech, the code is brought out in action in situations that demand swift action. In order to maintain the public order, the orders are issued and the broadcast of such perverse content is banned. The issue once again arose in the year 2016, where a channel; 'Peace TV' was being telecasted even though it not seek any permission to get broadcasted in India and was not even registered. It was banned as there was probability of the content being filled with speeches that could incite violence and create disharmony between communities. So as to air in India, registration is an essential requisite. This was a clear violation of Rule 6(6) which makes it illegal for any broadcaster to cast his content without being registered with the government.[18]

4.3.1.1 Constitutionality of the Programme Code

Keeping in mind the above mentioned points, it points out to one important question. Whether the Broadcasting body is under a public duty to prohibit or allow the content? Such proposition was discussed in the *Aamoda*[19] case wherein the apex court held that the body is not under an obligation to perform such task and it did not constitute public duty. The problem arose whereby telecast of telgu content was not being shown in the state of Telangana as the broadcasters who were a private entity stopped showing the content as it maligned the legislators of the Telangana state. It was alleged by the petitioner that such action violated his fundamental right to speech and expression. But the Supreme Court settled the position by establishing that the body that had stopped telecasting the content was allowed to do so since it was a private entity and not state.

Thus it can be concluded that the regulations so employed are used for curtailment of any form of hate speech but the problem lies in its administration. The excessive use of these regulations could have a negative impact as censorship has been held by critics as an unreasonable restriction upon free speech. The solution for this is the effective and timely implementation and acting on self regulatory basis and not under political duress.

4.4 Cinematograph Act

The Central Board for film certification can perform pre censorship of the films made under the Section 5B of the act and also order the expurgation of the films from the public domain under Section 5E of the act. Guidelines issued by the Central Board of Film Certification (CBFC) deal with restricting films and its forms for the prevention of hate speech being disseminated in the public sphere.[20]

The most important criterion to be adhered to while issuing the order of censorship is that the creation or the content should be seen in its entirety and not in portions. The in general impact of the work has to be examined as has been held in the *Anand Patwardhan*[21] case. The documentary made in this case did not constitute the criterion for censorship since the work did not have the possible effect of creating any communal divide.

In *Rakesh Mehra*[22] case, the Delhi high court had looked into the matter concerning the guidelines of the film boards and whether they were complied with by the appellant. It was challenged on the ground that the work violated certain provisions of the SC/ST act as there was a scene in which the lady cleaner was worked up by the police authorities. Contrary to all such contentions, the court emphasised that wok of the film should be seen in its entirety and not in portions. Furthermore, the scene depicted the atrocities faced by the minority communities and was meant as a message for ending discriminatory practices.

Most importantly, the work should be seen from the perspective of a ordinary prudent man who can take work or depictions in a courageous way and understand the context rationally and not from the perspective of men who are feeble minded and get hurt in matters that are different to their point of view.[23]

In the case of *MSG2*[24], there was a scene where the protagonist is portrayed as a saviour to the adivasis (tribal people) who are described as devil. The court pointed out that the citizens of this country have the ability to differentiate between what is real and what is shown as fiction or fantasy. The role of the protagonist was similar to that of a fantasy role as he was shown to possess unnatural powers. Such depiction is clearly something that can be deciphered by the viewers. Further, the term adivasis is not restricted to the scope of scheduled caste or tribe but has a very wide ambit.

If there is an anticipation of violence because of the content of the picture made, such movies cannot be subject to censorship if the people protesting the release of the film act in an extorting manner. With regard to this, the court has held that:

"If the film is unobjectionable and cannot constitutionally be restricted under Article 19(1), freedom of expression cannot be suppressed on account of threat of demonstration and processions or threats of violence".[25]

The court laid down that it is the primary duty of the government to ensure the fundamental freedoms are given predominance over such acts of intolerance and extortion by the fringe groups.[26]

In the case of Darma Sansad, Yati Narsinghanand and Jitendra Narayan Tyagi (formerly known as Wasim Rizvi) for delivering hate speeches at the religious conclave held between December 17 to December 19, 2021. Narsinghanand was refused bail in two cases: one for delivering hate speeches at 'Dharam Sansad,' and the other for making insulting remarks about Muslim women. He was charged with violating sections 295A and 509 of the IPC in the latter case. He said that Muslim women functioned as politicians' mistresses. He has been under judicial detention since January 16th.

4.4.1 Constitutionality

It is observed that movies have an engrossing viewership and brings out more emotions than other forms of entertainment. Therefore, this has to be seen from a different perspective and should have tests evolved for testing the act imposing censorship. Furthermore, the court has held that the restrictions imposed are well defined and there is no scope of ambiguity. When compared with the act, the regulations contained are in consonance with the Constitutional scheme. There is the need for censorship keeping in mind the greater interest of the society at large which comprises of diverse strata. Therefore, if such orders are issued and when complied with the essential rules and standards, it could help in prevention of hate speech.[27]

4.5 Press Council of India

It has been given legal basis by the act enacted in the year 1978 for keeping an over watch over the standards and the performance of the press and whether the journalist are acting within the scope of prescribed rules and regulations. There are certain provisions that entail the circulation of various news agencies and daily's in order to maintain law and order and curtail such content that could risk public order and tranquillity. This is provided under Section 14 of the act which empowers the council to act as a 'quasi-judicial' body. It is further seen that the council shall be composed of a chairman and other members which comprise of noted journalists, heads and editors of news agencies and such members shall be 28 in number. This is laid down in the Section 5 of the act[28]. Other than this the council has the power to censure the content which is shown to masses under the Section 14 of the Act.[29]

Before the council is approached with regard to particular content having the likelihood to create law and order problem, the complainant should approach the editor of the newspaper or the news agency. But the complainant may approach the council if the editor does not reply to his complaint or request; or the issue is not resolved amongst them. However, such complaint should be filed within the stipulated period of two months if it pertains to the newspaper and four months if it pertains to other mediums. The actions are of preventive nature, hence only reprimanding can be an option but definitely not any penalizing action.[30]

In 1996, there was a case that dealt with regulations of the council. Dainik Jagran which is a leading daily in the country was served a notice which was issued by the council itself. Such action was taken as there was a incident involving two opposing communities and the daily had carried the news in a manner that was in derogation with the rules and regulations of the act. But the contention that was raised on the part of their defence by Dainik Jagran was that the council had not followed the procedures and the lacked due to procedural impropriety. But it was stated by the council that it was their foremost duty to inform any newspaper or agency about any complaint that has arisen against them and such action is good in law. With the powers that are bestowed upon the council with the effect from 1979, it has transformed it from a mere regulatory body to a quasi-judicial body.[31]

[1] Germany Kent, YOU ARE WHAT YOU TWEET, Star Stone Press, (2015).

[2] *Shreya Singhal v. Union of India,* (2015) 5 SCC 1.

[3] *Ibid.*

[4] Section 69A, INFORMATION TECHNOLOGY ACT, 2000.

[5] Rule 5, Information Technology (Procedure and Safeguards for Blocking of Access of Information by Public) Rules, 2009.

[6] Rule 9(3), Information Technology (Procedure and Safeguards for Blocking of Access of Information by Public) Rules, 2009.

[7] *Ibid.*

[8] Rule 2(i), Information Technology (Procedure and Safeguards for Blocking of Access of Information by Public) Rules, 2009.

[9] *Shreya Singhal v. Union of India,* (2015) 5 SCC 1.

[10] *Ibid.*

[11] Apar Gupta, COMMENTARY ON INFORMATION TECHNOLOGY ACT, Lexis Nexis, (2015), p. 590.

[12] *Shreya Singhal v. Union of India,* (2015) 5 SCC 1, para 119.

[13] Apar Gupta, COMMENTARY ON INFORMATION TECHNOLOGY ACT, Lexis Nexis, (2015), p. 601.

[14] 189th Report, PARLIAMENTARY STANDING COMMITTEE ON HOME AFFAIRS, 2015.

[15] Rule 6, Cable Television Network Rules, 1996.

[16] *Ibid.*

[17] Ministry of Information and Broadcasting, *Warning issued to Sathiyam Channel*, 12th May 2015.

[18] Rule 6(6), Cable Television Network Rules, 1996.

[19] *Aamoda Broadcasting company v. Union of India*, W.P. No. 17389 of 2014.

[20] Section 5, Cinematograph Act, 1952.

[21] *Aamoda Broadcasting company v. Union of India*, W.P. No. 17389 of 2014.

[22] *Rakesh OmprakashMehra v. Government Of NCT of Delhi*, 197(2013) DLT 413.

[23] *Ibid.*

[24] *Prem Mardi v. Union of India*, WP (C) No 8883/2015.

[25] *S. Rangrajan v. Jagjivan Ram*, 1898 SCC (2) 574.

[26] *Ibid.*

[27] *K.A. Abbas v. Union of India,* AIR 1971 SC 481.

[28] Section 5, PRESS COUNCIL ACT, 1978.

[29] Section 14, *ibid.*

[30] Chapter III, *ibid.*

[31] *Jagran Prakashan v. Press Council of India*, AIR 1996 All 86.

CHAPTER FIVE

INDIAN PENAL CODE vis-a-vis FREEDOM OF SPEECH AND EXPRESSION

5.1 Introduction

Freedom of speech and expression is a two edged sword and while it provides the citizens the enjoyment it also prohibits certain acts that could tantamount to abuse of this intrinsic and inviolable right. Sedition is an offence under Section 124A of the Indian Penal Code that attracts mass public criticism on the pretext that it violates the sacrosanct right to free speech and expression. The background of Sedition has been dealt in Chapter I of this work while this chapter tries to bring out the grounds on which the constitutionality of this provision is challenged. In this chapter the emphasis is on two things, the post independent phase and validity of the existing legal framework concerned with sedition and the abuse, unthoughtful and insensitive use of this law. Since the attainment of Independence, this provision has garnered media attention and criticism of liberals and legal luminaries among others.

Apart from this various law commission have presented their reports that have dealt with the issue of sedition and the reform this section needs. Apart from the reports, in 2018, the commission presented a consultation paper in which it tried to reason that this provision does not hold good in the present 21st century and now can be scraped out. Other than the commission, former Supreme Court Justice A.P. Shah has highlighted that this provision is an encroachment upon the freedom of speech and expression and there are other provision enacted that can deal with offences relating to national unity and integration.

5.2 Law Commission on Sedition

The Law Commission of India has deal with the issue of sedition and the reform this provision needs in its report as early as in the year 1968. Reports followed in the year 1971 which comprised of two reports pertaining to this issue and in recent times in the year 2017 when the commission made a distinction between the ingredients of the offence of Sedition and hate speech.

5.2.1 The 39th Report, 1968

This report basically dealt with the penalty that was imposed under this offence and pointed out that the punishment prescribed for this particular offence was too grave and disproportionate to the object sought to be eliminated. It highlighted that this offence should not be made punishable than imprisonment for life as there are certain inconsistency in the manner the cases are prosecuted with regard to the offence of sedition.[2]

5.2.2 The 42nd Report, 1971

This report in particular propounded major suggestion to this provision and emphasised on the fact that the mental element should be included as an ingredient to the offence of sedition. Furthermore, the disaffection that is limited to the government should extend to its other organs such the Judiciary and even the Executive. The major premise of this report was that it limited the scope of punishment to seven years accompanied with fine as it pointed out towards the gap present between the imprisonment for life and three years imprisonment. It is to be noted that the Union government did not adhered to such recommendation at that time. In the year 1971, another report was published which has presented the recommendations made out in the 42nd report only.[3]

5.2.3 267th Report, 2017

In the year 2017, the commission brought forth the recommendation on the issue of hate speech which established the distinction between hate speech and sedition as an offence. The premise of this lies on the fact that the former happens to be an offence that hampers the public peace, while the latter is a grave offence which includes the act which cause threat to the 'sovereignty' and 'unity' of the nation. There are various tests devised to check which form of speech qualifies to be held as seditious as what may seem to be 'disaffection' or 'disloyalty' may rather be constructive criticism and point out the legitimate short comings that are prevailing in the society. There exists a 'right to offend' which must not perish to the colonial provisions as speeches which may seem to be offensive may later prove to be path breaking in the form of ideas and expressions forming the basis of a healthy modern democratic society.[4]

5.3 *Interpretation of the Offence of Sedition*

It has been precisely laid down that the provisions of this law are only brought into play when there is an incident which involves violence due to the speeches made. The public order test is the foremost requirement to invoke this section. This above mentioned proposition has been emphasised by the Supreme Court in the *Kedar Nath*[5] case which has interpreted this section in a careful manner. On one hand, there is the most sacrosanct idea of country's sovereignty and unity while on the other hand there is the intrinsic right of free speech. The apex court has tried to construct in a harmonious manner this problematic scheme and has held that only in cases where the speaker or person accused intentionally or penchant disrupts the law and order of a public gathering by the provocation to cause violence. This particular position of the court's interpretation has stood the test of the time and holds well in the present scenario as well. The court laid down the following keeping in mind the citizen's intrinsic and inviolable right to express themselves in a free manner.

"the security of the State, which depends upon the maintenance of law and order is the very basic consideration upon which legislation, with view to punishing offences against the State, is undertaken. Such legislation has, on the one hand, fully to protect and guarantee the freedom of speech and expression, which is the sine quo non of a democratic form of Government that our Constitution has established. ... But the freedom has to be guarded against becoming a licence for vilification and condemnation of the Government

established by law, in words, which incite violence or have the tendency to create public disorder. A citizen has a right to say or write whatever he likes about the Government, or its measures, by way of criticism or comment, so long as he does not incite people to violence against the Government established by law or with the intention of creating public disorder".[6]

But the above scheme has been given a cold shrug by the lower judiciary as well as the executive and misapplication of this section by the government has led to violation of not only the inviolable and unalienable right to speech but also of human right violations due to unprecedented arrests. With this we shall look into the cases where there authorities have misread the provisions of this colonial law.[7]

5.4 1947 to 21st Century

The *Manubhai Patel*[8] case is a classic example dealing with the confiscation of the book that contained material which propagated the philosophy of a communist leader, namely: 'Mao-Tse-Tung'. This was carried out following the provisions contained in the criminal procedure code under Section 99A. The divisive book contained content that included speeches and other incidents that preached about communist ideology as devised by various Chinese philosophers. The book was confiscated on the ground that it had the likelihood of inciting violence in the country and attracted the penal provision of Section 124A of the IPC.

However, where the executive and the legislature disappoint the alleged offenders, the judiciary comes in play in upholding the principles of fairness and reasonability that are intrinsic to a fair trial. The Gujarat High Court in this very case came to rescue and declared that this particular book did not in any way tend to cause disruption of public order and furthermore, did not in any manner tries to undermine the government in power.[9]

The court further laid down that the book only contained ideas and expressions that gave a glimpse of various principles that the communist party follows in their country. Hence, such book did not in any manner have the propensity to subvert the government in power and in finality quashed the orders of the Gujarat government against the accused person.[10]

Similarly, if a person makes out appeal to the people during the election campaigning that whether they are content with the manner the elections were carried out that consisted of the bourgeois election, does he has the probability to get booked for the felony of sedition. This situation arose in the *Aravindan*[11] case as the accused person was framed under various stringent provisions of the penal code including sedition. The court in this matter was not satisfied and held that the proceeding was still awaiting any action to be taken by the Magistrate and went on to quash the frivolous allegations made out against the accused.

There is an important aspect of this particular provision that in order to constitute the commencement of the proceedings against the accused, the permission of the government has to be taken prior to any action against the accused person. The Andhra Pradesh High Court in the *Kandi Reddy*[12] case pointed out this discrepancy where the petitioner was framed on the charges of sedition without the prior sanction of the State Government. The prior sanction is of great importance as it is only through the proper channels that the prosecution can be initiated under section 196 of Cr.PC. The court citing this discrepancy set aside the case pending against the petitioner.

In another case that involved the chanting of slogans was that of *Balwant Singh*[13]. Balwant Singh along with Bhupinder Singh was charged with the offence of sedition who were both serving under government departments. They both came near a movie house and started hurling slogans in support of an extremist group. This incident had taken place just after the news of the assassination of then Prime Minister; Smt. Indira Gandhi had taken place. Following this incident they were arrested and prosecuted. They were successfully convicted for the said offence and awarded prison sentence of one year along with fine. They went on to appeal against this decision to the Supreme Court which over ruled their conviction and emphasised on this issue in the following words:

"the raising some slogan only a couple of times by the two lonesome appellants, which neither evoked any response nor any reaction from anyone in the public can neither attract the provisions of Sedition and causing enmity or hatred between class of persons..... Some more overt act was required to bring home the charge to the two appellants, who are Government servants. The police officials exhibited lack of maturity and more of sensitivity in arresting the appellants for raising the slogans. Raising of some lonesome slogans, a couple of times by two individuals, without anything more, did not constitute any threat to the Government of India as by law established not could the same give rise to feelings of enmity or hatred among different communities or religious or other groups".[14]

Thus, it can be understood from this above proposition laid down by the court that mere chanting of slogans would not attract the essential postulates laid down for the offence against the state. Furthermore, it emphasised on the working pattern and efficiency of the police authorities and held that these instances can be defeat the very purpose for they were enacted and portray the role of state in a negative manner.[15]

There was another case that showcased that lack of efficient application of such severe penal provisions leads to subverting of the fundamental rights of the citizens and not the subversion of government in power. This incident was related to the conviction of Bilal Ahmed who was linked to an extremist outfit which had its primary objective of separation of Kashmir from India. This was a grave charge levelled against an Indian citizen. He was alleged to have given inflammatory speeches in the heart of the state of Hyderabad in India to young men and furthermore, was said to have provided them the means to undergo combat training.[16]

It was discovered that he had weapons of military grade and had offered the same to the youth. Another charge that was levelled against him was that he had incited the populace about the inhuman treatment that was being imparted to people in Kashmir by Indian forces. He was charged under various provisions of IPC and the Arms act along with prevention of terrorist act.[17]

The court referred to the 1962 position and re-iterated the important element related to sedition as pointed out in the judgment and further observed which is mentioned as follows:

"*Sedition has been described as disloyalty in action, and the law considers as sedition all those practices which have for their object to excite discontent or dissatisfaction, to create public disturbance, or to lead to civil war; to bring into hatred or contempt the Sovereign or the Government, the laws or constitutions of the realm, and generally all endeavours to promote public disorder*".[18]

It was then decided by the court as so to overturn the judgement as the provisions of sedition cannot be invoked due to various factors. Firstly, it was the untailored manner in which the trial court had convicted the said person without going into the provisions which demanded evidence and the decisive ingredients that were needed to achieve a precise and undisputable conviction. Secondly, the absence of any patent instance that could show the manner in which the accused was involved in provoking citizens against the sovereign. Hence, he was convicted for other penal provision such as under the arms act and not for the graver offence of sedition.[19]

5.5 21st Century to Present

There are numerous instances where the mere criticism or pointing out flaws in the government machinery and its mechanism of governance has led to people getting booked under this offence. Many journalists and other media personnel have been framed for doing their work of finding out the flaws and discrepancies in the system. The true essence of a modern state democracy lies in the transparency that it offers and not in the authoritarianism it sponsors. Some of these instances are mentioned in the following pages.

The twin tower bombings were a major event in the 21st century and later on this tragic event led to declaration of war by the United States. Following this, there was an incident where some scholarly group of people were arrested for handing out pamphlets to people which mentioned that the twin tower incident is comparable to the American nuclear attack on Japan and Indian government should not have supported American cause for war. They were booked on sedition charges as 'relationship with friendly nations' is a reasonable restriction upon the inviolable privilege of free speech. But the rationale behind such content was that the United States got the taste of its own medicine as in both incidents thousands of innocent people had lost their lives.[20]

The above situation only sparks the debate that whether a strict reading the bare provision going to achieve the ends of justice or whether a liberal interpretation going to pave the way forward for a healthy democracy.

Another such incident is of a scholar who went ahead and criticised the government and chief minister of Gujarat state for his late action during the Gujarat riots menace. Apart from that she had criticised the manner in which the authorities had dealt during the communal violence that took place. She had expressed these views as a social campaigner in the print media such as 'Indian Express'. A F.I.R. was registered against the daily for carrying such news under the provision of section 124A. Although later on these above levelled charges were withdrawn.[21]

The above instance only points out to one thing which is lack of conformity with the Supreme Court's decision in the *Kedar Nath*[22] case and many more such cases have occurred where the lower judiciary have not abided by the rationale developed by the apex court. There is a distinction between the government itself and its organs. Criticism of the former is an element for invoking provision and not the latter. Also the most important factor being the incitement to commit violence is absent in most of the cases. When the intent is absent then how come the executive cast such charges upon its own countrymen?

Writing or predicting about the outcome of the elections is a part of normal routine editorship or creative writing. But in matter where the alleged person named Dr. Ashish Nandy had written an article about the possible result of the elections that were to take place in the state of Gujarat. He was framed under the charges for promoting enmity between classes and the offence for making certain contention about the nation. The Supreme Court in this matter instantaneously came down heavy on the manner and the pretext on which the said accused was charged with such grave charges. The court went on to observe that there were plenty of other happenings in the country that warranted for such action and not this one where the mere critical analysis of an election outcome was in question.[23]

5.5.1 *Arundhati Roy and Geelani Issue*

There was a public event that was held on 21st October 2010 in Delhi regarding the issue of Kashmir. The issue of 'Azadi' was the highlight of the event as the key speakers namely, Syed Ali Geelani and Arundhati Roy highlighted the alleged human rights violation in the problematic State of Kashmir. The event was basically held so as to demand the release of political prisoners that were arrested by the security forces.[24]

The problem of this entire event was that there were continuous allegations of human rights violation in the state of Kashmir by the speakers at the event but the media had presented the views expressed by the speakers in an aggravated form. The media presented the views so expressed as being too extreme and seditious in nature. It has been expressed by the apex court that views expressed however inflammatory they may be but if they do not incite violence are held to be not seditious. But this ended up in a different domain as the topic attracted media and public attention which added to the disadvantage of the speakers.[25]

Arundhati Roy who happens to be a booker prize winner and a notable writer expressed her views by stating that Kashmir was not a integral part of the country and it was a matter that was pending in the United Nations. She expressed her concern over the anti-naxalite movement that was in progress by the Indian government. She further stated that the state of

Kashmir was militarised by the Indian security forces and it needed enough breathing space. She equivocate for the liberation of Kashmir from the colonial like Indian government's rule. Moreover, she extended her support to people of Kashmir and their fight for 'Azadi' but posed a question to them as to what was the cause they were really fighting for. Towards the end of the speech she mentioned that how the people of Kashmir have come out in open extending their support for the kashmiri pandit and their plight and saluted the women and the younger generation of the Kashmir about their struggle for independence.[26]

With regard to the views expressed by Syed Ali Geelani, the chief guest of the event in question were also held to be seditious. He had extended the view of the above mentioned speaker and added further to it. He said that the Indian forces had killed lakhs of Kashmiri and raped women. Citing one of the examples of such alleged instance where two Kashmiri woman were raped by Indian military personnel and were later held to be as death by drowning in pool which happened to be only few feet deep. He further expressed that the continuous struggle for independence cannot be curtailed by the use of force. He cited the killings of kashmiris and ended by saying that their struggle would continue.[27]

These above mentioned speeches and views were widely criticised for being against the country's interests and there was hue and cry in public domain with regard to holding these persons liable for their act of expression. One of the citizens ended up filing an F.I.R. in Delhi's Tilak Marg police station. The request for the same was denied by the station house officer as he mentioned that the key ingredients of the offence of sedition were not present and hence did not entertain the request for filing the F.I.R. as the views expressed were by not by itself seditious but showcased the mindset of the people of Kashmir.[28]

The complainant by the name of Sushil Pandit then approached the magistrate seeking redressal of his denied request and filed a complaint under section 156 clause 3 of the IPC. The complaint was converted into a F.I.R. on 27th November 2010 and made it evidently clear that the police authorities had to begin their investigation into this probe and submit with the magistrate the status report of the same. The people accused were charged with the offences under sedition, promoting enmity between classes and mischief provisions under IPC. Another section that dealt with unlawful prevention act was also invoked upon these persons. However, there was never a charge sheet filed and the persons who were allegedly accused of the above stated offences were never arrested. Furthermore, investigation was held to be as inconclusive.[29]

There exists various viewpoints with regard to the issue of Kashmir problem and people with different views express accordingly. The media for that matter cited the views expressed in the event as being treacherous and anti Indian. A sort of media trial had taken place and the overall image of the entire incident had been placed into the minds of Indians as being an act of Sedition. But it turned out to be opposite as the speakers there never intended to uproot the government and did not in any way show that their intention was to incite the public gathered there to commit violence. If one sees this incident through the judgment of *Kedar Nath*[30], it appears not to be seditious.

5.5.2 Binayak Sen Issue

Dr. Binayak Sen is a practicing paediatrician who was also involved in humanitarian and social activism. With more than 25 years of experience in the field of providing medical aid to poor and needy, he was also involved in criticism of highhandedness of the government in the operations led by the Indian paramilitary forces against the naxalites in the region of Chhattisgarh. He was also the general secretary of the People Union's for Civil Liberties (P.U.C.L.) state unit. He was one of the foremost critics of the *Swala Judum* movement which is a government action against the naxalites in the state. Along with this movement, the government has also enacted a draconian era like legislation namely, Chhattisgarh Special Public Security Act, 2005 which had certain anomalies that were being pointed by the P.U.C.L.[31]

This social organisation had demanded the in depth enquiry into the anti-naxal operations due to certain procedural and other failures. It was during this time that Binayak was threatened to drop all the allegations else the Special enactment could be used against him and it is ironical that this very act was used against him. There were other two main accused in the offence of possessing material that posed threat to the nation's sovereignty and integrity. Narayan Sanyal who was already a convicted felon was being treated by Binayak for his ailments in the Raipur Jail. They both had met more than thirty times. Piyush Guha was the arrested person that revealed everything in a chain of events.[32]

Dr. Binayak was charged with the offence of sedition and other grave offences including waging war against the state. He was accused of furthering the naxalite propaganda through the aid of other two main accused. Sanyal was the member of communist extremist organisation that had been involved in several destructive incidents in the state.[33]

The trio was charged and prosecuted for the above mentioned offences and were convicted later on. The accused persons pleaded not guilty and kept on applying for bail. The judgment had been arrived based on certain anomalies. The first one was the lack of evidence that was ignored while they pleaded in the court. The second one was that there was discrepancy in the affidavits filed in the High Court and then in the Supreme Court. The place of arrest of one Guha was mentioned different in both the affidavits; hence there was lack of moral ground which was covered under the pretext of typographical error.[34]

Later on, the apex court granted bail to Binayak and suspended his sentence after looking into various anomalies in the judgment of the Trial court. The court held that there was not enough evidence that could prove the accused being a so called naxalite but he was in reality only a sympathizer to the cause of the extremists. Furthermore, the court pointed out that mere possession of naxal literature would not constitute the person liable for the offence of sedition in the same manner that a person who might possess a book on Gandhi would not make him as a Gandhian.[35]

5.6 Recent Trends and Efficacy of Sedition Law

Another illustration, where sedition has been misused or abused is one of Aseem Trivedi case whereby a cartoonist was arrested by the police authorities under the stringent section of IPC; section 124A, the now unconstitutional 66A of the IT Act and also under section 2 of the Prevention of Insults to National Honour Act. The accused cartoonist was charged because he made certain objectionable cartoons that upset the tone of many in the government as well as other watchful citizens. The case was filed by Amit Katarnayea who happens to be a Mumbai based lawyer as he was offended by the manner in which the cartoonist had sketched out the cartoons. The tone of sketches in question was corruption and portrayed the Indian National Emblem in a distinct unusual manner by showcasing wolves instead of heads of four lions.[36]

The court brought forth a distinction between criticism and disloyalty and further observed:

"*disloyalty to Government established by law is not the same thing as commenting in strong terms upon the measures or acts of Government, or its agencies, so as to ameliorate the condition of the people or to secure the cancellation or alteration of those acts or measures by lawful means, that is to say, without exciting those feelings of enmity and disloyalty which imply excitement to public disorder or the use of violence*".[37]

This proposition lays down what has been said even by the apex court in many cases let alone many other high courts in plenty of matters. In recent times, where one of the cabinet ministers went on to criticise the judiciary and its approach with regard to the reforms in the collegium system of the appointments in higher judiciary was also charged for the offence of sedition. But the Allahabad High Court did not entertain this charge and held that it was merely a criticism and did not in any manner intended to disrupt public order or create violence. It was held by the court as follows:

"*Hence any acts within the meaning of s. 124A which have the effect of subverting the Government by bringing that Government into contempt or hatred, or creating disaffection against it, would be within the penal statute because the feeling of disloyalty to the Government established by law or enmity to it imports the idea of tendency to public disorder by the use of actual violence or incitement to violence*".[38]

The rationale for striking down this colonial law is because of the manner in which it is being casted upon the citizens of this great nation. If people that belong to a particular locality and in their periphery a nuclear power plant comes to be soon established thereby causing their displacements, then don't they have a right to protest against such happening? Apart from the issue of displacement, lack of rehabilitation facilities from the government and the threat it poses to their surrounding and in many cases to their livelihood is something that is understandable to any ordinary prudent person. But it turns out this was not in the case of Tirunelveli district, where the people were protesting the establishment of Kudankulum nuclear power plant and were booked under the offence of sedition. There is no clarity as to the most important question: did the state government authorise the initiation of proceedings which is the foremost requirement to be fulfilled for prosecution under this offence. Other than this, there are countless people who have been put in the F.I.R. as accused even though the veracity as to their committing the act or not through any evidence is far from clear. This is also evident from the fact that there have been no charge sheet framed so far and it was only until the Supreme Court intervened that some names were dropped from the F.I.R. but some still remain and the overall efficacy of this question only points in direction of scraping off this law.[39]

In one of the most recent cases, on 12th April 2019, the Kerala High Court overruled a special court verdict of conviction of four persons who had been convicted for the said offence as they had organised a meeting of the banned terrorist organisation "SIMI". The National Investigation Agency (NIA) had charge sheeted sixteen persons out of whom, two were awarded sentence of life imprisonment while other two were awarded a sentence of twelve years. Astonishingly, one of the accused was a juvenile who was later dropped out of the case after the high court entertained the appeal.[40]

The Court went to hold that the speech may have been made out maliciously but there was nothing seditious in its contents and held as follows:

"*None of the speakers said that they should show disloyalty to the Government of India. They were projecting the plight of Muslims, of course viewed in a narrow angle as saviours of Muslims community. They might be wrong in making such a statement. It is their thought process that the rule of Mughal or Nizam is better and they should fight under the leadership of SIMI. Therefore we are of the view that none of the accused can be charged with the offence under the Section 124A of the IPC*".[41]

Thus one thing can be seen from above mentioned case laws that the point where the criticism becomes uncanny to the government in power, it comes heavy handed on its critics. However, it is no new principle that constructive criticism is essential or rather vital to a healthy democracy but still what makes it more questionable is the intent with which the government takes the actions making it even more questionable about the viability and existence of this provision anymore.

JNU incident is what one can term as Kohinoor for the opportunist Indian media that has given it undue media attention and driven away from the rationale mindset that our country has been known for. The shouting of anti India slogans and creating an environment that is supporting a neighbouring country's ambitious policy of infiltrating terrorists and de-stabilising the country is in no way protected. Rather such instances belittle every little sacrifice made by thousands of freedom fighters who fought hard for country's independence. Every citizen has a fundamental duty that though not enforceable by courts, serves as a guiding principle for the country's young and agile youth. Such duty is provided under Article 51A (a) which casts upon us a duty to uphold the nation's constitution and the ideals and institutions it comprises of. Although the case is pending in court, slogans that were shouted tantamount to subversion of the government and demeans the very ideals and principles enshrined in our Constitution which we strive to achieve.[42]

5.7 Conclusion

Sedition is an offence that has been used since the colonial times as a means to encroach upon the citizen's inviolable and intrinsic right to freedom of speech and expression. This was achieved by framing various freedom fighters for this offence and hence the Britishers were successful in keeping them at bay from continuing their fight for Independence. But this particular provision has been cast upon Indian citizens in the post-Independence era in a haphazard and careless manner. This has caused unrest amongst the Indians as well as the legal critics and luminaries as they have stressed upon the deletion of this provision. They have further stressed upon amending the provisions present under other enactments so to maintain the unity of the nation as well as the faith of people in the Indian democracy.

[1] Gulshan Bawra, UPKAR, 1967.

[2] LAW COMMISSION OF INDIA, 39th Report on: "*The Punishment of Imprisonment for Life under the Indian Penal Code*", 1968

[3] LAW COMMISSION OF INDIA, 42nd Report on: "*Indian Penal Code*", 1971.

[4] LAW COMMISSION OF INDIA, 267th Report on: "*Hate Speech*", 2017.

[5] *Kedar Nath Singh v. State of Bihar,* 1962AIR 955.

[6] *Ibid.*

[7] Shivani Lohiya, LAW OF SEDITION, Universal Law Publishing Co. (2014), p. 54.

[8] *Manubhai Patel v. State of Gujarat,* 1972 Cr LJ 388.

[9] Shivani Lohiya, LAW OF SEDITION, Universal Law Publishing Co. (2014), p. 55.

[10] *Ibid.*

[11] *Aravindam v. State of Kerala,* 1983 Cr LJ 1259.

[12] *Kandi Reddy v. State of Andhra Pradesh*, 1999 (1) AP LJ 405.

[13] *Balwant Singh v. State of Punjab*, (1995) 3 SCC 214.

[14] *Ibid.*

[15] ShivaniLohiya, LAW OF SEDITION, Universal Law Publishing Co. (2014), p. 56.

[16] Batuk Lal, COMMENTARY ON THE INDIAN PENAL CODE, Orient Publishing Co. (2013), p. 551.

[17] *Ibid.*

[18] *Bilal Ahmed Kaloo v. State of Andhra Pradesh*, AIR 1997 SC 3438.

[19] Shivani Lohiya, LAW OF SEDITION, Universal Law Publishing Co. (2014), p. 57.

[20] *Ibid.*

[21] *Id.*, at p. 58.

[22] *Kedar Nath Singh v. State of Bihar,* 1962AIR 955.

[23] Batuk Lal, COMMENTARY ON THE INDIAN PENAL CODE, Orient Publishing Co. (2013), pp. 551-553.

[24] K L Bhatia, CASES AND MATERIALS ON CONSTITUTIONAL LAW OF INDIA, Universal Law Publishing Co., (2016), pp.631-703.

[25] *Ibid.*

[26] Shivani Lohiya, LAW OF SEDITION, Universal Law Publishing Co., (2014), p. 65.

[27] *Ibid.*

[28] *Id.*, at p. 66.

[29] K L Bhatia, CASES AND MATERIALS ON CONSTITUTIONAL LAW OF INDIA, Universal Law Publishing Co., (2016), pp.631-703.

[30] *Kedar Nath Singh v. State of Bihar,* 1962AIR 955.

[31] Shivani Lohiya, LAW OF SEDITION, Universal Law Publishing Co., (2014), p. 68.

[32] *Ibid.*

[33] *Ibid.*

[34] *Id.*, at p. 71.

[35] *Binayak Sen v. State of Chhattisgarh*, SLP (Cr.) 2053/2011.

[36] K L Bhatia, CASES AND MATERIALS ON CONSTITUTIONAL LAW OF INDIA, Universal Law Publishing Co., (2016), p. 689.

[37] *SanskarMarathe v.State of Maharashtra & Anr.,*(2015) Cri LJ 3561.

[38] *Arun Jaitley v. State of U.P.,* 2016 (1) ADJ 76.

[39] Anushka Singh, SEDITION IN LIBERAL DEMOCRACIES, Oxford University Press, (2018), p. 57.

[40] *Union of India through NIA v. State of Kerala &Ors,* CRL.A.No. 12 of 2016.

[41] *Ibid.*

[42] *Kanhaiya Kumar v. State of NCT of Delhi,* W.P.(CRL) 558/2016.

CHAPTER SIX

OPINIONS AND SUGGESTIONS

When we use the term freedom of speech and expression phrases such as two-edged sword and two sides of the same coin come into play. The reason for using these phrases is that one needs to understand the importance of such right and the responsibilities that come along with it. Speech comprises of many elements and one of them is dissent or rather criticism upon a certain point of contention. Such criticism is to be based upon rationale approach that is supposed to result in a constructive resolution of the problem that resulted in such criticism.

Dissenting is held to be the essence of a progressive democracy but such opinions should be based on some rationale, something that speaks for itself. But when instead of using a rationale approach, one goes on to criticise in a manner that negates progressiveness and moreover acts in a detrimental manner, such criticism sprouts out wide problems. Such problems could include within its ambit hatred, resentment, enmity between the citizens and in worst case scenario; violence. It is these reasons that one fears absolute free speech and thus paves way for reasonable restrictions to be mounted upon speech which deem necessary for a country like ours.

Indian Constitution is an epitome of human values and embodies the best of the elements that instill in a progressive society. From the chapters discussed in detail, it can be pointed out that the essence of free speech and its elements is clearly present in our constitution. The instrument of our rights prescribes certain restrictions upon exercise of rights which are certainly required keeping in the diverse social structure that our country comprises. Therefore, the contention that restrictions are wrong does not hold out well and the reasonable restrictions imposed under Article 19(2) are valid.

The issue of Hate Speech has been discussed in detail in this work. It is to be pointed out that where there are communities that have in the past had incidents imitating inimical approach over their mannerism, lifestyle and thoughts, there will be friction. One cannot negate this premise and has to take into these factors while enacting legislations. The same has been done since the colonial times as depicted by provisions inserted into the penal code to deal with these matters. However, these should not favour any one particular community. These provisions are only brought into action when the intent with which the speaker is communicating his thoughts is malicious and detrimental to the well-being of the society at large. The penal provisions have time and again come in handy and have resolved peace and tranquillity in the Indian society and have provided equal protection to all including the minorities that are present in our country.

In Indian context, one has to be examine that hate speech cannot be in any way given the same protection as the United States has given in its country. This is based on the fact that the country came into being after the amalgamation of more than five hundred scattered states. Keeping this position in mind, one has to find the common breeding point between the threat that hate speech poses and the impairment caused to one who cannot express oneself freely. Thus, there is a long way for the Indian society that has wide diversities to take in the incendiary speeches to be a part of one's way of communication.

The International aspect of the issue of hate speech only enlightens us that the Indian legislative system is not lagging behind in promising rights to the citizens. India is signatory to many such conventions and covenants. Many of these statues resemble the scheme of our Fundamental Rights as our own scheme is based upon the equitable and righteous ancient philosophy as well as the modern concept of human rights which has prevailed since time immemorial on this soil.

When it comes to expressing one's convictions and ideas in the online sphere, there is high probability of misinterpretation of one's thoughts. This has led to unprecedented problems and cases related to online hate speech. There are groups and pages that specifically promote content on their platforms that disseminate hatred in the society. Such incidents have been reported and dealt under the provisions of Information Technology Act. But convicting someone only because their thoughts are not in conformity with others does not justify such action. Only when there is likelihood of violence or when there is evident provocation for committing violence, only then such provision be levied.

In any egalitarian and democratic society, one cannot be always expected to conform to the majoritarian opinion as this would be antithetical to the idea of equality. Ideal such as patriotism cannot have strict interpretation and can vary as per the prevailing situations and one can express the love for their country in their own manner. Some may chose to get involved in constructive debates and disparage the government's policies while others may shy away from doing the same. While indicating certain pitfalls in the government machinery, one may end up using discordant and unpleasant language. But this does not mean that the discontentment be labelled as sedition. Such stringent provision should be sparingly used and only when the intent behind such speech or action is to cause disruption or to cause violence by unlawful means in order to overthrow the government.

Number of incidents give concrete evidence pointing towards one main thing that the nuance of dissent is something that our country has lacked although we comprise of multitudes of diversities. We have nothing but displayed strength and resilience during grim times than invoke provisions of sedition against our own countrymen.

There are varying opinions and if one is discontent with the government in power and its policies or if one speaks about the country not rising up to the expectations of the women or calling out the nation as chauvinist, does not in any way acts against the idea of a nation. Berating certain features or some peculiarities by indulging in positive criticism cannot tantamount to sedition. India has struggled long for its freedom and if one does not have the right to criticise in a free country then there won't be any distinction between the colonial time and the 21st century.

In the present era, the sedition laws are not meeting the objective for its very existence. It has been used as per the whims and caprice of the government in power to curb any voices that threaten their political ambitions. Therefore, in order that nation prevails over inhibitions of any regional party or fringe groups, this law should now be scrapped off and amendments be made to existing penal provisions in order to make them further potent and in consonance with the growing needs of the society.

Morality and decency evolve with the societal changes and needs. Therefore in the garb of sovereignty, one cannot equate one's thought to be demeaning than others only because they don't meet the societal standards. Only when hatred and enmity is caused with malicious intent, then only can the person be charged with concerned offences.

Keeping the above views in mind, I would now like to draw certain suggestions with regard to hate speech and sedition laws highlighting the need for reforms and discrepancies that may perhaps help in resolving the issues.

Suggestions

Our legislature has been accused by various critics for sleeping over important issues. The same legislature has in recent years dealt with certain propositions and recommendations that deal with the issues at hand. With a view to take out our country out of its colonial mindset, certain proposals have been initiated in the Parliament through the mechanism of private member bill. One of the members of Rajya Sabha had posed such reform in 2011 by taking the stance that Sedition law be ousted. This is to be done as this same law has been used on numerous occasions for curtailing the Indian freedom fighters basic right to peaceful protest including the inviolable right to express oneself through speech.

Four years after this above mentioned proposition, another private member bill was initiated which suggested that this provision should be modified to that extent that only violent acts and provocation to violence is used as a ground for charging someone under this law. This suggestion is in line with the various judgments that have time and again cited Kedar Nath judgment for dealing with the offences relating to sedition. It has been abolished in United Kingdom, the very country that enacted it in India.

India is progressive democracy and it is in a nascent stage of striving towards becoming a developed nation. India as a nation has come far from its colonial structure and mindset and needs to question the efficacy of enactments that represent colonial mindset. In the present scenario this law has been used to curb the citizens in exercise of their basic rights. There are plenty of other laws and special enactments that are potent enough to deal with elements that tend to threaten the sovereignty and integrity of the nation. Some of the following suggestions would support my contentions:

i. Sedition Law should be scrapped off as the objective for which it was enacted ended with the Independence of India. It has been abolished in England more than a decade back so that it ceases to be known for enacting draconian laws.
ii. Till the time it is not ousted, certain modifications should be made. Scrutiny of the F.I.R. should be done by a specially enacted committee under the aegis of High Court to be formed in every State in order to siphon frivolous and vexatious complaints meant to satisfy personal vendettas and curb dissent. This would act in furtherance of achieving the ends to justice and serve the larger public interest in play.
iii. Damages in the form of compensation should be awarded to those 'discharged' of the offence. This would uphold the human rights principles enshrined in our Constitution and act in furtherance of country's commitment to various International covenants as well as to organisations.
iv. Time period should be fixed for the trial of proceedings in matters relating to offences against State.
v. Arrest in cases related to these issues should be made only after a specialised body gives approval. At the moment prior approval of state government is required to initiate proceedings for offences related to hate speech and sedition. In cases where arrests are made in spite of prior approval not being granted, such matters should be given primacy while awarding damages.
vi. Hate speech laws under the IPC should be reviewed and inclusion of certain words be carried out to fill the gaps created if provision for sedition is deleted from the code.
vii. There is requirement of enactment of more stringent provisions to deal with the issue of online hate speech.
viii. Terrorist prevention enactments to be made more efficient by amending provisions to incorporate speedy trials in order to send message in the society to anti-national elements.
ix. IT Act to incorporate more strictness against intermediaries. Intermediaries to act swiftly against elements involved in spreading negationism and totalitarianism on online platforms.

The above suggestions are made keeping in mind the fragile and nascent stage the nation is in. Laws need to accommodate the requirements of the time and when the requirement has been fulfilled or it ceases to exist, then such enactment should be scrapped off or modified to accommodate the present needs. All laws relating to imposition of restrictions upon citizens rights should be casted keeping in mind the consequences that result from such restrictions.

www.ingramcontent.com/pod-product-compliance
Ingram Content Group UK Ltd.
Pitfield, Milton Keynes, MK11 3LW, UK
UKHW021922190726
13853UKWH00002B/788

9 798886 411614